About the author

A regular contributor to *Advertising Age,*
Richard A. Payne graduated Phi Beta
Kappa from Princeton University and holds
an MBA from the Harvard Business School.
He has held important marketing positions
with several major companies and has,
over the past decade, shown thousands of
people *How to Get a Better Job Quicker.*

HOW TO GET
A BETTER JOB
QUICKER

How to Get
a Better Job
Quicker

RICHARD A. PAYNE

New York / Taplinger Publishing Company

41655

First published in the United States in 1972 by
TAPLINGER PUBLISHING CO., INC.
New York, New York

Published simultaneously in the Dominion of Canada by
Burns & MacEachern Ltd., Ontario

Library of Congress Catalog Card Number: 71-164584

ISBN 0-8008-3963-3

To Judy Hanrahan
whose kindness and inspiration
made this book possible

CONTENTS

Frustrated! Does that word describe you? It will apply to a great many people who first turn to this page. There are many reasons why you could be frustrated. Maybe you see a long wait before your next promotion. You may not be paid as much as you think you should be paid. Maybe you feel you've outgrown your present job and that there is no line of advancement for you. It simply may be that you recognize your potential, while the company you work for does not. It really doesn't matter why you're frustrated. As long as you are, this book will make good reading.

The fact that you opened this book suggests something else about you. In going after a new job, you'd like some help. There are lots of reasons why you might want it. You may be thinking about changing jobs for the first time, or for the first time in a long time. You may have been trying to get a new job for many weeks or months without the success you thought you should have. Whatever the case, you'd like a little help, some practical, down-to-earth guidance. And, you have the initiative to seek it out. If this is the case, read on. This book is all about one simple idea: How to get a better job quicker.

"A better job sounds nice," you say to yourself, "but what do you mean by 'better'?" You can be sure it doesn't mean a better vacation policy or health insurance plan. Nor better hours or a company cafeteria. A better job is a job in which you'll make more money. Twenty per cent more. Maybe twenty-five. A better job is one in which you will have greater responsibility, a greater opportunity to learn, and a greater potential for future growth. Isn't that what you want in a better job? That kind of job is not as difficult to secure as you might think. At least it won't be after you finish reading this book.

If you agree with my definition of a better job, you still may question the word "quicker." This book will try to provide you with the skills you need to get a job in one-third less time than it would take a less-well-informed job-seeker. If you're not in a hurry, this book will still make your job search easier and faster. A tough promise to meet? Yes. But a realistic one because this book provides you with the tools you need to seek out and get a better job. Did you ever try to complete a project without the right tool? Such as using pliers when you needed a socket wrench? After you struggled with pliers for an hour, you borrowed a socket wrench, and in a few seconds you did what you simply couldn't do with a makeshift instrument. Because this book provides you with the right tools, tools that have worked time and time again, you'll realize that getting a better job quicker is a real, attainable objective. No idle promise. No pie in the sky. What are the tools you need to get a better job quicker?

• A knowledge of the fundamentals of self-selling. Ninety per cent of the job-seekers I know have the personal qualifications that will make them most desirable job applicants, but fewer than 10 per cent know how to present these assets to prospective employers.

• The knowledge of how résumés can and should be used to work harder for you. A résumé is infinitely more than a record of your past. It can be *prima facie* evidence of why you are better than your competition.

• A format and approach which make even difficult interviews pay off. So obvious, once you know them. So valuable you'll kick yourself for not knowing them sooner.

• The basics of writing letters that will make you stand out as the one candidate your prospective employer wants most. Most of the job-seeking letters sent today aren't worth the postage to send them.

If your objectives are in tune with the goals of this book, and you're open minded enough to at least explore techniques you have probably never heard of before, read on. But let me warn you, a once-over-lightly reading of this volume won't get you a new job—won't get you anywhere near it. You have to make this book work for you. You have to spend the time required to apply personally the techniques outlined in this book. Don't expect miracles. To make this book work you'll have to spend hours developing each phase of your campaign. You and you alone can decide whether it's worth the time and the effort. Lest you lack determination to tackle this approach, remember that the techniques found in this book have helped thousands. They can help you to get a better job quicker.

HOW TO GET
A BETTER JOB
QUICKER

INTRODUCTION

Are You Ready
to Go After
a Better Job?

PUTTING YOURSELF IN THE RIGHT FRAME OF MIND

Three years ago one of the best-known advertising agencies in New York City lost its largest account—an airline which spent over $25,000,000 on advertising each year. The next day 360 people, out of a staff of 800, received notices that their jobs had been terminated as of the end of the month. Three hundred and sixty good men and women thrown into the street on a single day. Three hundred and sixty experienced, capable people left on their own to seek jobs in a remarkably small industry. The scramble for available positions was unbelievably fierce. A year later many were still without work.

Let's hope the odds against you are not as tough. Even if they're not, it would still be foolhardy to think getting a better job is a breeze. A survey several years ago showed that the average job is sought by nineteen people. That means you are, in all probability, competing with eighteen others. Your résumé will rest silently on the desk with a stack of résumés of men with qualifications fairly similar to your own. Your prospective employer will sit, hands folded, looking at nineteen men dressed in their neatest suits, each talking fast and hard, seeking to impress the man behind the desk that he should be the one.

What are the men like who will compete with you? There's a good likelihood that some will be more distinguished-looking than you. Some will speak more eloquently and fluently on their feet than you do. Some will have gone to a "better" school than you did. And, to make the game just a little bit more difficult, you don't know who your competition is. You don't know what weak spots they might have that you could match yourself against. You've got to play the game on your own.

If this sounds like a pretty tough nut to crack, these facts should make it seem just a little bit tougher. Your prospective boss is not eagerly awaiting you. Chances are he'll look over your résumé (along with eighteen others) at the end of a hard working day. If the first man to see your résumé is in personnel work, your résumé may be just another piece of paper to shuffle on his desk. Even if you make it past round one and, on the basis of your résumé, you are invited to cross the threshold of your prospective employer's office, the sledding won't be easy. You'll have only a few minutes to convince the man behind the desk that you're the man he should take on. Even if he gives you a half-hour or an hour of his time, chances are what he learns about you in the first few minutes of your interview will convince him that he should proceed further, or that he should let you politely off the hook. Still feel like going on with the job of getting a better job? Well, there's one more thing I should re-emphasize. It will take a hell of a lot of effort and a hell of a lot of energy. Count on spending one hour for every year you've spent in business, determining how best to sell yourself; another half-dozen hours polishing a résumé that will get you in the door. Twenty-five more hours searching out the names and addresses of those companies you might like to join and those executives whom you should try to see. And then there are the interviews. You can easily spend three hours on each, if you count your transportation and waiting time. So if you interview ten companies twice—there's another sixty hours of effort and energy on your part.

Putting it the simplest way I know, getting a better job quicker is one of the toughest jobs you'll ever face. It takes time, organization, a lot of elbow grease. And it's a very lonely challenge. No one will hold your hand. No one will do it all for you. If you're frustrated enough with your present job, you'll be glad to make the effort it takes. Lots of people I know aren't willing. Going after a better job is just too much trouble for them, so they settle for the status quo. What about you? Are you ready to fight for your next step up?

DO YOU KNOW WHAT YOU WANT FOR YOURSELF?

On the very first page, this book promised to help you land a better job. Better in several basic ways: greater financial rewards, greater responsibility, and a greater opportunity for personal growth. The funny thing is that a better job (as defined) might not be better for you! If the new job won't make you happy, if it isn't what you want to do, if it leads you away from your long-term career objective, you could hardly call it better. Before you apply the techniques outlined in this book in earnest, then, you had better first wrestle with the problem of what it is you want to do in your next job. There is, after all, not much sense in running fast without knowing in which direction you're heading.

When you're deciding what's right for you at this stage of your career, be down-to-earth, objective, practical. Don't delude yourself into believing that what you ultimately want is "to be president of a *Fortune* 500 company." That sort of objective is so pie-in-the-sky that it can only serve to mislead you. Instead, review what next steps people at your current stage of career development can practically hope to succeed to. Then select the one or two attainable job positions that you'd like to shoot for. After you have decided on the attainable position you want, think about the kind of company you would like it to be in—small, large, or in between. And where you would like to live.

At this point, you might raise this thought: "Supposing I'm really not sure what I would like to do. A number of jobs would appeal to me. Then what should I do?" The most simplistic answer to this question is this: Don't think about leaving your current job until you have a damn good idea of the kind of work you would like to have. Changing jobs is no flip business. Prospective employers don't admire men who change jobs every year. In a way, changing jobs is like changing wives. It can be done, and done successfully. But there is something suspect about the man who has had eleven wives. And his twelfth one will be a shy bride.

Quite frankly, this book does not dwell on career goals and the ways you can decide what's best for you. It presumes you know what you want . . . and are willing to strive to get it.* After all, this book has a single-minded purpose—to provide you with the tools you need to get the job you want . . . quicker.

---

* If you want help in deciding on your own interests and aptitudes, you can get professional advice for very little money. For three dollars the American Personnel Guidance Association will send you a list of guidance counselors who will give aptitude and interest tests for under $150. Their address is 1607 New Hampshire Avenue, NW, Washington, D.C. 20009.

1 How to Make the World Want You

FOUR PRINCIPLES OF SELF-SELLING

At one of the first classes I ever gave on the subject of "How to Get a Better Job Quicker," I asked each person present to come forward and tell the rest of the class why we should hire him or her. A distinguished-looking, gray-haired, vested gentleman in the class offered us this answer as to why we should hire him:

> You should hire me as your next plant manager because I'm responsible for all phases of manufacturing in the company where I am now, including production, purchasing, scheduling, plant engineering, and industrial engineering. I've been involved with computerized inventory control, production-control systems, warehouse locater and inventory systems, and budgetary control systems. And I've had a total of fifteen years' experience with four of the leading companies in my field.

On the basis of his presentation, I asked the class whether they would hire this distinguished candidate. The first few classmates to speak said, "Yes"—because of the gentleman's appearance. And then one member of the class said, "No. I know the kind of experience he's had. But I don't know if he's any good at what he's been doing." This classmate was right. Soon the rest of the class was on his bandwagon. Looks aside, for all we knew, the distinguished gentleman may have bungled every assignment he ever had in the many areas of manufacturing in which he's worked. We knew he had fifteen years of experience with four companies. It's equally possible he left each of these just as he was about to be fired. What's missing from this distinguished gentleman's presentation that could have convinced us he's worth hiring? A simple statement of what he had accomplished at each of the companies for which he's worked.

There are four basic principles in selling yourself. The first and most important principle to believe in is this:

1 / *Your prospective boss doesn't care what you did between nine and five. He only cares what happened as a result of your being there.*   In a word, it isn't a laundry list of job functions that turns on the men who might hire you. It's what specific things you were able to get done that in some way improved your company's situation.

At the very same class, another, somewhat younger man told us why we should hire him. His reasoning was altogether different. Here's what he told us with a great deal of enthusiasm.

> You should hire me because I've got tremendous machine and fabrication know-how. I'm thoroughly familiar with a wide range of metal, plastic, and fiberglass tooling techniques. And, I've got genuine administrative perception. I have a full grasp and working knowledge of a broad cross-section of manufacturing and planning controls. And I'm a real morale and productivity builder. I'm adept in planning and organizing, scheduling and follow-through to make sure we get the job done. Not only that, I'm a profit producer. I can help any manufacturer beat the cost squeeze.

At the end of his speech, a few people in the class volunteered that they'd hire this bright-eyed, bushy-tailed young man. But most of the class felt differently. Most, like me, wouldn't have hired the second executive either. The reason: because, while he told us he was good (damned good, I might add), we had only his word for it. As someone said to me after the class, "Not only did his speech sound extremely boastful, but I really didn't know whether what he was saying was fact or fiction."

In point of fact, none of us in the class that night knew whether the young, animated man's evaluation of himself was accurate. It's possible—perhaps probable—that his opinion of himself was a biased one. The second important principle of self-selling, then, is this:

2 / Your prospective boss isn't interested in your opinion of yourself. He doesn't know you. He doesn't know how well you evaluate yourself. What your prospective boss wants is evidence that you are the best man he can hire. How can he get this evidence? With results. With accomplishments. Things that you did that the other eighteen candidates with whom you compete didn't do, or couldn't do. Your prospective boss needs to be convinced. The one thing that will convince him most is specific accomplishments that might have a bearing on his problems.

"That's all well and good," you say, "but how do I know that the results I achieved on my old job, or my last several jobs, are the kind of results my prospective boss is seeking?" There's a simple answer to that question: You don't. But it doesn't matter. On the priority scale, your prospective employer must rate experience secondary to something else, your ability to get the job you have to do done. And you can prove your ability to get results by describing the things you achieved at the job you now hold, or previously held. Don't get me wrong. It's nice to have the exact experience your prospective boss is looking for. But it's not essential. If you've done well at whatever you have done, you're far better off than the man who may have the (in quotes) exact experience but who has done nothing on his current job to prove he has the ability to take on the one he's going after. To put it in its simplest terms, if you have demonstrated accomplishments on a smaller job, you can handle a bigger job. Believe it because it's true, and go after the bigger job.

If you doubt that experience is secondary to accomplishment, consider this example: A number of years ago a friend of mine, then a sophomore in college, wanted to apply to Harvard Business School. He wrote to the dean and asked what subjects he should take in order to get accepted at this, the most famous business school in the country. The dean wrote back, "It doesn't matter which courses you take, just do well in what you elect to study." My friend majored in, of all things, philosophy—because he liked it. He ended up with honors in his field and a Phi Beta Kappa key. To no one's surprise, he was accepted at Harvard Business School even though he had never taken a course in marketing, finance, or economics.

When you stop to think about it, it's quite natural that accomplishments on the last job are more important than precisely right experience. Why so? Because in a year's time what you have learned on the new job will be infinitely more important than what you learned in five years on the last one. In point of fact, you may need to overcome some of the experiences you picked up at your former company simply because they don't tie in with the procedures and systems that are in effect at the company you hope to join.

Even more impressive to your prospective employer than accomplishments are a series of accomplishments that show progressively greater responsibility and progressively more important results. I know a man who is today the executive vice president of a major health-aids company. He is responsible for the world-wide marketing of fifteen famous products with multimillion-dollar sales. How this gentleman moved into the marketing field demonstrates the importance of progressive accomplishments. He began his career in the accounting department of an appliance company. His first job was in Accounts Payable, first as a junior accountant, then as accountant, then as senior accountant. All in the space of three years. At this point in his career he decided he was more interested in marketing than in accounting. Thwarted in his attempts to get into marketing at the appliance company, he decided to seek employment elsewhere. He managed to secure a fairly senior job in the advertising department of the health-aids company he now presides over. How? By selling his rapid rise in responsibility and progressive accomplishments in the accounting department of his former company.

3 / Consider your career in terms of a series of progressively more important accomplishments. Some may be minor, others major, in terms of the new job that you seek. This is the third basic principle of self-selling. Organize them in such a way as to show this growth quickly. Help your prospective boss to know that you can be counted on for personal growth. Make him believe you are a man on the way up, a man with potential for his own job.

Concerning this third basic principle, I am often asked, "But supposing I haven't had a series of progressively more responsible accomplishments?" My answer to this question is dogmatic. Virtually all of us make greater contributions with each passing year—if for no other reason than that we have more experience. It then becomes a question of presenting your contributions in such a way as to build the concept of progressive accomplishments in the eyes of the man who may hire you. Take the purchasing agent who is asked to talk about his business career at an interview, for example. He might talk about his successes over the last year as a purchasing agent. He could, on the other hand, tell his boss that he started in the business as an assistant buyer. A year later, after saving the company money on a particular job, he was promoted to buyer. Two years later he was chosen to become an associate purchasing agent because of an accomplishment along the way. And now, five years later, he is a purchasing agent. By focusing for a few moments on the small, you can make your current situation look larger.

At this point in time many of you may be experiencing doubts. I have stated that the first and most basic principle of self-selling is that you sell your accomplishments. Not your experience. Not your opinion of yourself. I then asked you to sell your accomplishments in a progressively more important manner, whether in a résumé, an interview, or letter. Now you may well be wondering what so many others have wondered: Is this type of self-selling bragging? Is it just plain boastful? I will confess to you that when I first considered the concept of accomplishment-selling I felt embarrassed to boast about the things that I had done. I knew darn well that I wasn't the only one responsible for the successes of some of the business ventures in which I had participated. And I felt awkward saying, "I saved the company thousands of dollars," or, "I introduced a new product line that increased company sales by two million dollars." If you have pangs of conscience as I did about boasting (and it wouldn't be surprising if you did), then bear with me as we pursue the fourth basic principle of self-selling.

4 / *Selling your prospective boss on your accomplishments is not bragging if you present the problem and your solution to the problem in a factual, honest, and anecdotal fashion.*   Here are some examples of anecdotal accomplishment-selling taken from real life. See if they sound to you as if the authors are bragging:

> After four years of successive sales declines on product "X" I developed, then recommended to management a new package concept for this product. Management accepted the recommendation, and the Purchasing Department secured the package for us. Nine months after the new package was introduced, product "X" sales were 8 per cent ahead of the previous year.

> The cash balance at our company was extremely low, and management contemplated a major bank loan. After analyzing accounts receivable, I recommended a cash discount for prompt payment. Management bought the idea. The new discount improved our cash position to the point where a bank loan became unnecessary.

> Recommended utilization of a new glue formula in the labeling ma-

chine to overcome a label-sticking problem. This suggestion increased labeling speed by 20 per cent and reduced machine overhead by an equivalent amount.

Would you think seriously about hiring the men whose accomplishments appear above? Do you think they were bragging? The first man told us there was a packaging problem with his company's products and that he recommended a change. Obviously, his boss, and perhaps his boss's boss, had to buy his recommendation. The change wasn't his alone, and he never claims it as such. Yet he was instrumental in the change, and his contribution is obvious. The second example came from a financial man, and the third from a production engineer. In my view, none of the statements sounds boastful, since they are businesslike presentations of specific problems and the real life solutions recommended by the men involved. In short: accomplishment-selling, if handled right, is the strongest way of proving your worth. It is not tooting your horn.

Even if you buy that accomplishment-selling is not bragging, you may have one further doubt. It might express itself like this: "My job is the kind of job where I haven't made any contributions, and I can't make any contributions." You will never convince me of that. Let me tell you a true story that explains why. A man who worked for one of the world's largest advertising agencies came to see me one day. He had spent fifteen years in the media department, and in a management shuffle he was fired. We went over the concept of accomplishment-selling, and he said the same thing you may be thinking, "I have no accomplishments of note." I wasn't convinced, so we sat there for two hours, with me firing questions at him to try and stimulate his thinking. "Absolutely no contributions," he maintained the entire time. "None." And at the end of two hours, just as my patience was beginning to wear thin, I noticed that he was wearing a Little League tie clip. I asked him about it. He told me he had started a Little League in his home town in New Jersey. He started with only two teams. Now there are ten. He persuaded someone to donate a ball field and someone else to donate the lights. He organized a parents' committee. He had done this all himself. After talking about the Little League, I pointed out to him that he was a man of considerable accomplishment, that it wasn't bragging to talk about these contributions. And then the floodgates broke loose. Not all his business accomplishments were great. But they were accomplishments, nonetheless. And once I got him over the initial hurdle of talking about them, he was psychologically ready to talk about them in interviews. And in no time at all he found a better job at another advertising agency.

There you have it. The four basic principles of self-selling:
1. Don't sell what you did between nine and five, but rather what you accomplished as a result.
2. Don't place a value on your own worth. Let the results of your efforts speak for themselves.
3. Sell your accomplishments progressively to show personal growth.
4. Tell your accomplishments in a factual, anecdotal form and they won't sound like bragging.

We could stop this book here. You have the guts of the matter. But as we go on, I will try to show you how to apply these four basic principles in your résumé, how to utilize them in your interviews, how to make them fit into your letters.

Now, let's turn from theory to a practical matter. How are you going to get your accomplishments written down in such a way that they provide the basis for selling yourself? It isn't easy. As I've said before, you may spend an hour for every year you've been in business. There is only one way to get your accomplishments written down, and that's to start now. List the successes, or near successes, you have had, the changes you have suggested and the results of those changes. It doesn't matter if you saved your company $10 or $10,000. It makes no difference, as long as you tried to save money and succeeded. Maybe you located a single customer for your company. The fact that you went after the customer and succeeded in getting him is what counts—not how many customers you went after. Maybe you created a design that won an award. That's an accomplishment, and your prospective employer should know about it. So now is the time to stop reading this book. Pick up a pencil and start writing down your accomplishments, the things you contributed to the businesses with which you've been associated—the things that you are proud of. Before you start, however, let me suggest a way of jotting them down for the first time. Write each as a story. First state the problem as clearly as you can, then state what you did about the problem, and, finally, state what happened as a result. Here's an example:

Problem. The cold cream we were selling looked sloppy when our customers opened the jar.

Solution. I suggested a cooling tunnel so that the cold cream would be set hard prior to capping.

Result. The product today looks much better than it ever looked in the past, and consumers have written to tell us so.

When you have finished writing up the ten or twelve contributions of which you are most proud, put your list aside for a day or two. Then return to it with a fresh eye. See if you can cut down your words to the absolute minimum. Take a look at the example above. Here's how we might reduce the words and make our statement of accomplishment more cogent and more effective:

Eliminated sloppy fill problem on cold-cream jars by recommending new cool fill production process. The change resulted in immediate increase in consumer acceptance of product.

Candidly, you won't find it easy to reduce your original accomplishment statements. There always seem to be words that you must leave in. Yet it is to your advantage to reduce to an absolute minimum the statement of problem, solution, and result of solution. Your prospective boss is looking at the résumés of eighteen other men besides your own, and he hasn't time to waste. If you can demonstrate that you are a man of many accomplishments in just a few short sentences, you're a leg up on your toughest competition.

To make your self-selling really effective, reduce your accomplishments to pithy, direct, positive, and to-the-point statements.

One word of caution when you write up your accomplishments: Make sure they sound believable. Don't claim to have done the impossible single-handed. It's easy to make yourself stand out, even as part of a group responsible for a project's success. To do so, just follow these two suggestions:

• Put your accomplishment in its proper perspective.
Here's an example:

> Initiated a program to switch from metal to plastic containers for our products. This change (in conjunction with a reduction in labor worked out by our manufacturing group), increased net profits 28 per cent the year following the shift from metal to plastic.

• Give credit to others, where appropriate:

> As a member of the president's financial task force, conceived a new costing system. This system was adopted as part of the overall financial program recommended by the task force to top management, and is in use today in three company divisions.

HOW TO RANK THE SALES POTENTIAL
OF YOUR ACCOMPLISHMENTS

If you have done your homework between the sections of this chapter, you have written down a number of your most important accomplishments—your contributions to those companies where you worked and those organizations with which you've been associated. You've tightened them up, reduced the verbiage so that in just two or three clear sentences your contributions are obvious, immediately apparent to anybody who might read them. And what you've said you've done is believable. No one will accuse you of being boastful or of being Batman. By this time, your wife or a friend may have read over your paragraphs to make sure it is clear, in the abbreviated version, what you contributed during your years in business. But there is another key question that has to be answered about your accomplishment statements: Are they relevant to the needs of your prospective boss?

Obviously, without knowing who your prospective boss might be, it is difficult to make sure the accomplishments you describe to him are important. There are, however, several kinds of accomplishments that are more important than others in the eyes of most successful executives. These are outlined below. As you look over this preferred list, keep your own accomplishment roster in mind.

• Profits. If there's one common denominator all businessmen understand, it's profits. Quite possibly you were reluctant to mention your contributions to profits because they may have been small ones. Mention them anyhow. Not every man is in a position to add a million dollars in profits to his company's coffers. I know of a man who, after seven years with a company, could report that he had saved his company only $17,000 in excess interest charges. The size of your personal profit contribution is less important than your ability to recognize an opportunity to increase profits at all.

• Increased Sales. You don't have to be a salesman to have helped increase your company's sales. You may have introduced a potential client to your firm. You may have corrected a pricing error which could have cost your company the loss of a customer. As a result of your production ideas, you may have contributed to a decrease in product cost which in turn resulted in a lower price to consumers. That lower price may have resulted in increased sales. You may have engineered a product improvement that helped the sales of a product. It doesn't matter whether you are in production, finance, marketing, or research, etc.; you have opportunities to help your company increase its sales. Let your prospective boss know about your contributions, no matter how small. Because, in the end, increased sales (with profits) are the aim of every business.

● Reduced Cost. As with increased sales, reduced costs are not the exclusive franchise of any single department. If you are a process engineer, chances are you reduced the cost of a manufacturing system. If you are in purchasing, you may have made an extraordinary buy that saved your company money. If you are an office manager, you may have improved an administrative procedure so that you didn't hire an extra girl. Prospective employers are looking for men who know how to save money. Because, ultimately, reduced costs become increased profits. If you've saved your company money, let it be known.

● Establishment of New Objectives and Strategies. I know a man who joined a great old New England company that produced a limited line of five products. Within a year after joining, this man had persuaded management to introduce three new product lines. Three months later my friend decided to leave in a dispute with management over the introduction of additional new products. At the time he prepared his résumé, results were not yet in on the success of the three new product lines he had introduced to the trade. He could not, therefore, refer to increases in sales and profits on his résumé. But his résumé was strong nonetheless, because he said in it: "Introduced three totally new products for the XYZ Company, the first introduced by this company since 1933."

● Successful Personnel Training. A man who attended one of my classes complained to me that he wasn't getting anywhere. As a claims supervisor in an insurance firm, he had trained no less than four men who had gone on to become vice presidents of the company. Yet he himself remained as a claims supervisor, with no corporate title. As he discussed his future, I suggested to him that he focus on his ability to train. His résumé now sports this accomplishment: "Developed successful training techniques which have resulted in advancing careers of four key Insurance Company officers." The ability to develop people is an extremely important asset which can increase the profits of the corporation for whom the trainer is employed.

• Recognition of Overlooked Problems. Recently I came across a résumé that said: "Analyzed costs and selling prices of three sizes of paints sold by the ABC Company. Discovered price structure, in effect for ten years, resulted in reduced profit to firm on larger sizes. Recommended price changes that increased profits on larger sizes while making it worth while for consumers to trade up to the bigger packages." This candidate scored well not only for his contribution to profits, but also for his curiosity, which led to the profit increase.

THE WORDS THAT SELL

Not all words create excitement. Take the difference between "hitting the ball" and "walloping" it. Certain words are active words; others are passive words. In talking about your accomplishments, try to use words that are exciting and active. Nothing annoys me more than a memo from one of the people who work for me saying, "Per your request, I am reviewing. . . ." I would much prefer the man to write instead, "This reviews the pressing problem concerning. . . ."

So when you talk about your accomplishments, let the words you select reveal your initiative, your extraordinary interest, your ability to move mountains. In this respect, try to use these words: initiated, developed, conceived, recommended, organized, analyzed, planned, presented, demonstrated, put into effect. There are other active, exciting words. This list only gives you an idea. Chose your own. But make sure each evokes a positive interest in you.

As a corollary, avoid words that suggest someone had to push you to do the job or that you were only following orders. Show your prospective employers that you are a man of initiative and action by using action-oriented words. You may feel that selection of words is a small point. Maybe. But for some men it has made the difference between "No" and "Welcome aboard." Don't be a runner-up.

2 | Ten Questions to Ask Yourself

This chapter is dedicated to those of you who haven't written up your accomplishments. It is a short chapter, but it may take you longer to get through than any other in the book. Because this is a chapter in which you take over, in which you do the work. If you have already written down a dozen contributions you've made and are satisfied that your prospective boss will be interested in them, you can skip this chapter. If not, read on.

This chapter is simply ten questions—plus a commentary on each. Before you read the questions, however, let me warn you. You may find yourself saying that you can't answer all or some of them. Your frustration at the difficulty of answering these questions may even lead you to doubt the validity of the techniques in this book. To put you at ease, let me tell you a remarkable incident that occurred in a class I once gave for a group of job-seekers.

Shortly after I handed out to the class a mimeographed sheet listing the ten questions I'm asking you to answer, one member (a tall blond man in the back row) raised his hand. When I acknowledged him, he exclaimed, "Your course on 'How to Get a Better Job Quicker' is no good!" "Why?" I asked. "Because," replied the tall blond gentleman with a strong foreign accent, "I can't answer any of your ten questions. So your course couldn't help me. So it's no good." I asked the gentleman to be patient and listen to other members of the class answer some of these questions. Throughout the class he remained silent, sullen, and unconvinced.

After others in the class had answered one or more of the questions, I asked the tall blond foreigner if he felt any differently. "Not at all," he replied. On the spur of the moment I said to him, "You have a strong accent. Where are you from?" "Czechoslovakia," he answered. "How long have you been here?" I asked. "Three years," he said. "And who taught you English?", I asked. "I learned it myself," he replied. "How?" I queried. "Well, I learned it while I was on the job." "Did you speak English at all before you arrived?" "Not a word," he said.

I pressed on. "Tell me," I asked, "how did you get out of Czechoslovakia?" "I escaped," the man answered. "Did you come alone?" "No. I managed to get my family out." "How?" I asked. "Well, I devised a scheme," the man went on. "I built a rubber life raft in my home. The Russians were very careful about where one traveled, but they allowed people to go to Yugoslavia for their holidays. My wife, two children, and I went to a resort town on the Adriatic, just across from Trieste. I had the rubber life raft, deflated, in a fake compartment of my suitcase. In the dead of night, I inflated the life raft and we floated fifteen miles to Trieste."

I turned to the class. "This incident tells a lot about this man. It tells us he has courage to start life anew in a foreign country with no knowledge of the language. It tells us he is creative. It tells us that he can organize and plan for an important activity. And it tells us that he can succeed."

Someone in the class suggested applause for the gentleman from Czechoslovakia, and this gentleman, who thought he couldn't accomplish anything, received a standing ovation.

The point of this story is simple. If you can't answer one or two or three of the ten questions in this chapter, don't be alarmed. It may be that you can answer other questions which are equally important because they show that you are a man who can accomplish difficult, if not impossible, things.

Now on to the ten questions that you should answer as best you can.

1 | Did you help to increase sales? How? How much? Be specific in your answer. By what per cent did you increase sales? How many dollars? What were the circumstances? What was your contribution? Did you help someone else to increase sales? What was your part in the sale?

2 | Did you save your company money? What were the circumstances? How much did you save? What was the percentage of savings? Was your ability to save your company money greater than that of the man before you in your job? Of other men in your company?

3 | Did you institute a new system or procedure in your company? Why? What was the situation that led to your instituting the change? Who approved of your suggested change? Did your procedure compete with any others? Why was it selected over others? What happened as a result of the change in procedure that you initiated? Has your procedure been adopted elsewhere in the company? Where? In other divisions? Departments?

4 | Did you identify a problem in your company that had been overlooked? What was the problem? What was the solution? Why was the solution overlooked? When you answer this question, you prove that you have the capacity to dig deeper than the next guy. And this is important. Let me illustrate. One of the men I coached worked as a market researcher for a company that markets a well-known women's bath powder. Over a few months he discovered a number of complaint letters concerning the powder's new fragrance. Yet the company had conducted a wide-scale fragrance test, and the new fragrance in the product was the one women greatly preferred over the previous one. Still the letters came in. Then he went digging. He found out that the fragrance in the powder was not the same one as the one that had won the test. What had happened was that an overzealous purchasing agent had talked to a different fragrance house, which promised him it could produce "an exact duplicate of the winning fragrance for about one-third the cost." On his own, the purchasing agent had substituted the so-called duplicate. Unfortunately, the duplicate broke down over time in the powder base. Hence the complaints. This story was a major factor in the market researcher's ability to get a better job. Have you demonstrated your capacity as a supersleuth? If you have, let all your prospective employers know it.

5 / *Were you ever promoted?* Why did your boss promote you? Was there some one thing you did that your management thought stood out? How many were in the running for the promotion you got? How long (or short) a period occurred between this and your last promotion? How much more responsible was your new job than your old? How many more people reported to you? The phrase "was promoted" is the only passive verb that is worth a damn in a résumé. It's proof that a third party thought you were better than your competition, that you had potential for growth. If you have been promoted several times by several different third parties, it is substantive evidence that you have potential for growth. Your prospective boss wants and needs to know this.

6 / *Did you train anyone?* Did you develop a training technique? What was this technique? What happened to the man or men whom you trained? How long was the training time by your technique as compared to the old one? What happened as a result of your training technique? Is your training technique

being used by others in the company? It's a well-known truism that men don't get promoted until they've trained a replacement. Employers are always on the lookout for men who know how to train the men to succeed them. If you're one of them, let it be known.

7 / Did you suggest any new products or programs for your company that were put into effect? What were they? Why do you think they were adopted? Did they result in extra sales to your company? Did you win any incentive awards? Did you develop any patents for your company? Did you win any industry awards for your company with your suggestions? Did you receive any extra bonuses for your product or program contributions? Did you represent your company at any industry-wide symposia at which your suggestions or programs were presented? Have your ideas for programs been published in any industry magazines or journals? Think hard for your contributions in this area. I don't know of a company that doesn't want to meet men who know how to innovate.

8 / Did you help to establish any new goals or objectives for your company? Did you arrive at these goals by any new or unusual thought process? Did you convince management it should adopt the goals you established? An executive I once knew was asked by management to take responsibility for integrating a newly acquired firm into his current company's operation. After six weeks' study of the methods of distribution of the newly acquired firm, the executive recommended that the new

firm not be integrated into the operations of the parent company. He reasoned that both the customers of the new acquisition and its methods of distribution were sufficiently different to make integration a hardship on both the acquisition and parent company. Management bought my friend's recommendation.

As a result of his personal goals, my friend decided to leave the company shortly after he wrote this report. Because of the timing of his move, he was unable to write on his résumé that he had "succeeded in building the sales of the newly acquired company." My friend's résumé, however, did include a statement that he had evaluated the acquisition policy of the parent company and recommended strongly to management that it operate the newly acquired firm independently. Management endorsed his recommendation. In this instance my friend sold prospective employers on his ability to evaluate and his ability to convince top management of the wisdom of his recommendations.

9 | *Did you change, in any way, the nature of your job?* Why did you redefine your position? How did you redefine it? Have other persons in jobs similar to your own had their positions redefined per your definition? Have there been any significant responsibility changes as a result of your redefining your job?

Whenever I think about the importance of redefining a job, I can't help remembering a young woman in one of my classes who told us the following story. She was a college graduate, an economics major. She graduated with honors. She wanted to work on Wall Street but was unable to get a job. (This took place before the days of Women's Lib.) And so she accepted a job as a clerk in the personal trust department of a large New York bank. Each day she added up figures, on the instructions of her immediate supervisor. One day, after a week on the job, she asked her supervisor why she was adding up the columns of figures. He told her. Then she said, "If that's what you want to find out, you're going about it the wrong way." She explained to her boss how she would approach the problem. A week later her title was changed from clerk to departmental statistician. Not surprisingly, at the time we met her in our class, she was head of the personal trust department. The essence of this case history is this: If you were able to redefine your job, broaden your responsibility, widen the scope of your authority, your prospective employer will be interested in knowing how you did it. Companies are continually seeking leaders. Men of sufficient ability to assume leadership positions don't come down the pike every day. If you possess the ability to shoulder more responsibility than other people in your position, let it come to the surface.

10 / Did you have any important ideas that were not put into effect? What were these ideas? What effect would they have had on sales or profits? Would they have led to extra savings? How did you develop these ideas? Why weren't they put into effect? The idea behind this group of questions is to turn each of your lemons into lemonade. Let me give you an example. A young man who worked for an advertising agency included on his résumé the fact that a product he helped to promote (a spray starch with silicones) did enormously well in test markets and would have been introduced nationally, were it not for a prior commitment on his client's corporate funds. A part of his résumé read like this: "Helped introduce a new spray starch brand into test market. After four months, brand secured first place position in this growing marketplace. Results were so well received by corporate management, tentative decision was made to introduce spray starch nationally. Limited funds, however, delayed national introduction." The fact of the matter is that the delay in introducing the product nationally was disastrous. The company's major competitor reproduced the spray starch with silicone formula and copied the advertising word for word and idea for idea, and the competitor's product was introduced nationally, but the original brand died in test market. Despite the sad ending, the man's contributions to the test marketing of a new product made good reading for his prospective employers. The fact that his plan wasn't used except in a test is no handicap to selling his original efforts.

CAUTION: Don't read any further until you promise yourself to answer these ten questions. And put your answers down on paper. Don't take a chance on forgetting them.

3 | How to Write a Stand-out Résumé

1 / What's a résumé? Most job-seekers I've met look forward to writing their résumés with fear and trepidation. They think résumé-writing is an extremely difficult job and one which they are ill-equipped to tackle. You, however, should be able to put together your résumé in a very short time, and with far less effort than you ever imagined, as long as you have completed and edited the list of accomplishments we discussed in the previous chapters.

All this chapter on résumés does is to help you highlight your accomplishments for your prospective boss and help you organize your contributions in a format and style that sells you fast and convincingly. What principles govern the format? The answer to this question lies simply in how you view your résumé. I hope you'll agree that your résumé is nothing other than a personal advertisement for you. If you accept this definition, then it follows that you should build your résumé around the principles that are basic to good advertising.

Unfortunately, in many meetings with people who have sought aid in writing their résumés, I have found a profound misunderstanding as to what résumés really are. Most people see them as no more than laundry lists or catalogues of their duties on past jobs. I guess this is because they think if they list their experience for a particular job, and it's (in quotes) suitable, they will automatically be granted an interview and a chance to sell themselves in person. Nothing could be farther from the truth. Today competition is so keen, and good jobs are so few and far between, that prospective employers don't have the time or inclination to meet all the people who are qualified. So employers use résumés to separate candidates with just experience from candidates with more than experience. Employers will look to your résumé to reveal: your ability to contribute . . . to get results . . . your ability to communicate problems and solutions . . . your ability to organize yourself.

Your prospective boss will be influenced not only by the content of your résumé, but also by its format and appearance. He will develop consciously or unconsciously a profile of you that will help him decide whether he should even consider you among the men he will ultimately choose from. At this point, you have already developed 90 per cent of the contents—your accomplishment list. Let's look for a moment at résumé format and appearance. Then at the end of this chapter we'll put everything together into a résumé that will turn on the men you want to sell yourself to.

2 / Is there a format for success? It would be nice if there were one unique résumé format that could be guaranteed to get you in the door, guide your interviews, and sell you up the line, or one outline that would get you the job you want. Unfortunately, such is not the case. Just as there is no single layout for great advertising, I have seen good résumés that use several different kinds of formats. Thus, I really can't put you on to an ideal résumé outline, even though I have a preference for one and will show it in detail later in this chapter. I can tell you this, however: Résumés that sell hardest have formats which embody the following principles.

RÉSUMÉ 1.

Resume of

Bryan Allyn Kent
44 Drawbridge Lane
Beaverton, Pennsylvania
Tel.: 206-475-1273

Age: 48   Height: 5'10"
Married: 3 children   Weight: 160 lbs

Education:
University of Wyoming, Laramie, Wyoming.
Graduated with a B.A. (Chemistry), 1943.

Job Objective:
To obtain the position of a Plant Manager or higher in the chemical or related industry. Solid foundation in plastics, rubber, pharmaceuticals and the ferro-alloy industry.

Product Experience:
In the plastic industry, vinyls, polyethylene, acrylo-nitrile-butadiene-styrene copolymers, silicones, polyurethanes and semi-conductor separators. In the rubber field, processing and use of all types of rubbers. Production of crystallines and antibiotics in the pharmaceutical industry. Production of ferro-manganese, silico-manganese, and ferro-silicon alloys.

Plant Experience:
Plastic coating lines, casting lines, high and low speed mixers, embossers, rotary printers, textile jigs and tenter frames. Rubber and plastic calendars, presses, extruders, various types of curing devices, fluid metering and mixing equipment, food saturating equipment. Chemical stills, centrifuges, solvent extractors. Electro-smelting furnaces, crushers, driers, heavy material handling equipment.

Employment Record:

May 1968 - June 1971	Unitrow Plastics Corporation - as General Manager & Director of Production. Manufacturers of vinyl coated fabrics.
April 1966 - May 1968	Special Metals, Incorporated - as Plant Manager. Smelters of ferro-alloys.
August 1961 - April 1966	Davidson Chemical Fabrications, Inc. - as Plant Manager and then General Manager. Manufacturers of styrene copolymers.
Sept. 1947 - August 1961	Hamilton Plastic Extracters, Inc. Manufacturers of plastics. Started as Development Engineer and worked up to Manager - New Product Development.
May 1945 - Sept. 1947	Johnstown Drug Company - as Product Chemist. Manufacturers of pharmaceuticals.

42

Duties, Abilities and Accomplishments:

As Director of Production, was responsible for production, maintenance, personnel, purchasing and production control. Reduced in-process inventory from seven weeks to two weeks. Improved labor rates, revised job classifications and yet reduced labor cost per unit produced. Was responsible, with the Treasurer, for setting up a computerized inventory control system for our raw materials and finished goods. Reduced accident rate by nearly 70%.

As Plant Manager of ferro-alloy plant, improved morale among the salaried foremen and corrected injustices in salary rates. Had the lowest, monthly unit cost of 50% ferro-silicon ever attained by any of the Canadian or American plants.

Joined Davidson Chemicals in 1961 as compound room chemist. A year later was made Plant Manager. Production was increased by 30%, scrap was reduced by 15%. Unit labor costs held constant in the face of fast rising labor rates. Was responsible for the plant layout of a new plant. Developed inventory control system for the parent plant. As General Manager, was responsible for all operations of subsidiary, Extrateen, Inc. Production increased further 13%. Reduced scrap 40%. Unit costs reduced 10%. Harmony was brought to a very troubled labor situation. Expanded system of complete inventory control developed for parent plant, to cover both plants and several warehouses in different parts of the world. Set up system so that it could be readily transferred to a computer when this became economically feasible.

As Manager of New Product Development, was responsible for the development of all new plastic products. This covered extruded, thermoformed, calendared, cast products and compression-molded solid plastics and closed cell sponges, fabric coating and paper impregnation. Given authority over both production and development, and increased profits by $250,000 over a 14-month period. Picked up excellent training in cost control, inventory control and industrial engineering.

As Production Chemist in a pharmaceutical firm, was responsible for taking new crystalline extraction processes from research laboratories working out details in the pilot plant and then putting them into full-scale production.

• Focus on results. Make accomplishments quickly obvious to the reader. Your prospective employer doesn't have time to seek out results. He doesn't have time to wait till the end to find them. Consider Résumé 1. There are no accomplishments on page one. None! Its author first details his accomplishments on page two. He presumes the prospective boss will take the time to get that far. He may not. In contrast, the résumé which follows (2)

RÉSUMÉ 2.

JAMES AUBREY ROBINSON
471 Old School House Road
Dobbs Ferry, New York
(914) HU 7-1578

Objective: National Sales Manager with a fast growing firm
distributing primarily through Food Chains.

1969--   SALES MANAGER
Tucker-Hamilton Corporation
Home Products Division
Morris Plains, New Jersey

Established Food Broker sales force

Obtained 82% all commodity distribution in original
markets on new floor care products

Appointed Manufacturer Reps and Master Distributors
in the professional floor care field

Supervised packaging graphics and distribution plan

Created promotional and marketing strategy

1966-1969   EASTERN REGIONAL MANAGER
U.S. Home Products Co.
Plastic Products Division
New York, New York

Achieved better than a 30% sales increase by
reorganizing region from 6 direct men, 5 brokers, and
2 distributors into a 30 broker, 10 distributor and
4 District sales manager sales force

Improved profits by decreasing small unprofitable
orders by 70% and increasing tonage by more than 33%

Secured and directed West Coast warehouse and shipping
point

Recruited for this position by well-known executive
recruitment firm

1964-1966   EAST CENTRAL REGION MANAGER
Lilac Foods Company
Los Angeles, California

Supervised $12,000,000 in sales through Food Brokers
and Grocery outlets

Responsible for the direction of sales trainees, office administration, and four public warehouses within region

Successfully introduced many new Lilac items including Liquid Lunch and "Skinnie" diet drink at both District and Regional level of responsibility

Promoted from Salesman to Chicago District Manager to East Coast Region Manager

1958-1964   ASSISTANT TO MANAGER--SUGAR SALES
D and H Foods Company
San Francisco, California

Successfully executed sales program for introduction of Sweet Touch sugar in major Northern cities of Columbus, Cleveland, and other major points in Michigan, Indiana, and Illinois

Sold powdered and confectioners sugar to chains and wholesalers in 10 states east of the Mississippi

Promoted from salesman to confectionary product specialist to Assistant to Manager of Sugar Sales

Education   1955-1957 Ohio University, General College
              1953-1955 Iowa, College of Education
              1969   SMI Field Sales Management Course

Military   Specialist 1st Class U.S. Army Quartermaster Corp.
            1951-1953

Personal   Age 37
            Married, 3 Children
            Excellent health

References   Excellent business, personal, and financial
            references will be provided upon request.

begins to detail accomplishments at the top of page one. Its writer presumed (and justifiably so) that he had better sell his accomplishments up front or he might never have a chance to sell anything else. Did you ever read an ad in which the headline didn't grab you first? The parallel is a telling one.

- Provide a very brief description of the job held, coupled with a statement of accomplishments in that job, rather than a detailed, dictionary-like description of the job, with no reference to contributions.

The writer of the next résumé (3) felt compelled to include a total description of every facet of his job function. On the other hand, the author of Résumé 4 briefly describes what he did and dwells on the results of his labors. As with great ads, this résumé sells the sizzle (your ability to contribute), not the size, weight, and cut of the meat (your experience catalog).

- Sell what's relevant to your reader. Compare Résumé 5 with the one you have just read (4). In Résumé 5 the author takes you through his education and early jobs before you find out what's happening *now*. The author of Résumé 4 did just the opposite. He lets you know what he accomplished yesterday because it's most relevant to your performance tomorrow. As a rule of thumb, your most recent experience is ten times more important to him than your experience five years ago. Not only should you talk first about it, you should talk most about it too. As a guide, if you've held four jobs, you might well devote 40 per cent of your résumé to your current job, 30 per cent to the previous job, 20 per cent to the job prior to that one, and 10 per cent to the one before that. Only in exceptional circumstances should you vary from that format. The obvious exception is the instance in which you desire to secure a job in a position more similar to your previous job than to your current one. In the advertising business, copywriters talk about primary and secondary benefits. Primary ones get the most play. In your résumé, your current accomplishments suggest your primary potential benefits to your prospective boss. Dwell on them in depth. The secondary benefits (your accomplishments five years ago) are frosting on the cake.

- Make it long enough to sell you, short enough to read. For

<u>RESUME</u>

1. MALCOLM W. CHISHOLM
   1374 Cannon Valley Road
   Ridgewood, N.J.
   Telephone No.: 201-572-8731

11. <u>QUALIFICATIONS</u>
    Thoroughly experienced in all phases of Plant and Manufacturing
    Management encompassing Industrial Engineering, Industrial
    Negotiation, Production Planning, Scheduling, Expediting,
    Machine Loading, Purchasing, Inventory Control, Plant
    Engineering, System and Procedure, Automation, Receiving,
    Shipping, and Security.

111. <u>BUSINESS EXPERIENCE</u>
     May, 1970 - Present   Paddleford Industries
                                         470-25 Bridge Street
                                         East Orange, N.J.

          Position Held: Plant Manager

          Function: Responsible for all phases of Manufacturing,
          including Production, Purchasing, Scheduling, Plant
          Engineering and Union Negotiation. We manufacture rigid
          expanded urethane products such as ceiling beams, plaques,
          switch plates and instant carving.

     Feb. 1969 - May 1970   Qualitone Manufacturing Corp.
                                         4770 Patterson Avenue
                                         Newark, N.J.

          Position Held: Plant Manager

          Function: Supervised all Manufacturing, Planning,
          Scheduling, Industrial Relations, Shipping, Receiving,
          Quality Control and Capital Appropriation. They manu-
          facture standard electronic components such as sockets
          supplying major national contractors like Levitt & Sons.
          Participated in the development of products for radio and
          television industries.

     April 1967 - Feb. 1969   Johnson-Dalton, Inc.
                                         Commerce Industrial Park
                                         Newark, New Jersey

          Position Held: Plant Manager

          Function: Direct all phases of Manufacturing, including
          Production, Personnel, Industrial Engineering, Union
          Negotiation and bidding on Government Contracts in
          diversified fields.

     Jan. 1965 - April 1967   Riverside Metals, Inc.
                                        Canal Street
                                        Newark, N.J.

          Position Held: Plant Superintendent

          Function: Managed all phases of Manufacturing, Plant
          Engineering, Quality Control, Automation, Scheduling

RÉSUMÉ 4.

RONALD SUMMERS   Married
358 Mill Spring Street   Two Children
Port Washington, New York   153 pounds; 5'9"
(516) PO 7-5613   Health good

JOB OBJECTIVE: Administrative responsibility in the marketing,
advertising, promotion of consumer goods

ADVERTISING
EXPERIENCE: Account Executive - J. Donald Cransdale Advertising,
1959-   New York
present

Full responsibility for Your Magazine Promotional
Account billing one million dollars. Promoted to
Account Executive on this account after less than a
year. Client gave outspoken endorsement to promotion.
Account has grown by one-third in past two years and
will increase by equal amount in 1961.

Assistant Account Executive
Part-time responsibility on Rock Springs Brewing and
Friendly Regular Coffee.

Originated and sold a creative approach currently
used in the Your magazine business paper campaign.

After conducting retailer and wholesaler interviews,
conceived a new marketing and advertising plan to
overcome obstacles in an intensely competitive Rock
Spring Sales District. Plan was accepted by
management and put into effect in this area. The
suggested creative approach to regional campaign has
been adopted for use in national campaign for 1962.

1958-1959   As assistant to Research Account Manager on the
Adams-Dover Account, conducted an exploratory market
study which was an important factor in Adams-Dover's
decision regarding an addition to its drug product
line.

Prepared a territorial sales analysis used as basis
for media allocations for Friendly Coffee in 1959.

Organized and headed fifty-man team which administered
the Cransdale Advertising Seminar Program attended by
over 500 persons. Program was judged by management to
be "The best run and best attended seminar program
ever conducted at J.D.C."

RÉSUMÉ 5.

JOHN H. GREERSON
1140 Camino Flores
San Jose, California 90412
213-437-6051

Age 39.   165 lbs.   Health excellent.

B.A. degree -   San Fernando State, 1953

Sept. 1953 - Feb. 1958 - Collegiate Drug Company

3 years Sales Representative.
2½ years District Manager.
Left Collegiate to go into packaging business, 1½ years.

Feb. 1961 - Nov. 1965 - Joined Murphion Corporation to head new
Industrial Division. Moved to Assistant to General Sales Manager and
then to Regional Sales Manager.

Nov. 1965 - Nov. 1968 - National Sales Manager - Developed sales and
sales force. Sales force grew to 60 and 4 brokers. Sales doubled.

Nov. 1968 - Promoted to head up new USA Test Market and moved to
Cleveland, Ohio. Responsible for sales in Michigan, Ohio and New York
areas - 17 brokers, assistant and 1 D.M. and 9 salesmen.

Jan. 1968 - Test market successful and moved to San Jose. As Regional
Manager 10 Western States. Company built new facility to sell packaged
instant potatoes. Hired 4 brokers to start and grew to thirty salesmen
and 3 District Managers covering California, Utah and Arizona. Obtained
solid distribution of company products in all retail outlets.

SUMMARY

Experienced in   - Hiring and training salesmen, district managers,
                    brokers.
                  - Sales to supermarkets, drug stores and department
                    stores.
                  - Setting up sales territories, programs, coverages,
                    etc.
                  - Budgeting, forecasting
Proven record of success

Compensation open for discussion, currently in low 20's.

most people, a two- to two-and-a-half-page résumé should be
more than long enough. Résumé 6 was a seven-page, handwritten account of its author's twenty years in business—so
laboriously long that neither you nor anyone else would have
read to the end, even if it had been typed.

RÉSUMÉ 6.

Ralph Carstair
143 Apple Valley Road
Seattle, Washington

Married, 2 Dependants
48 Years Old

From June 1969 To Feb. 1970   40 Hrs. Per Wk.   Layoff

Battleson Aircraft Company, Seattle, Washington.   Sup. Daniel Maloney,
Design Engr.

Mechanics Design Engineer   Aircraft Manufacturing   Start 225⁰⁰ wk
Final 240⁰⁰ wk

My Duties Included: Design, Layout And Detail All Component Parts,
From Tool Planning Request For The Manufacturing of Aircraft.
This Includes Assembly And Drill Jigs, Forming, Slings, Transportation
And Handling Dollies, Transportation Boxes, Etc.

From Feb. 1964 To May 1969   40 Hrs. Per Wk.   Better Opportunity

Astro General Corp., Los Angeles, California.

Sup. Paul Goldson, Senior Engr.   Structural Design Engineer

Aerospace Manufacture   Start 215⁰⁰ wk.   Final 225⁰⁰ wk.

My Duties Included: Developing Experimental And Production Designs
From Preliminary Design Data, Sketches, Or Verbal Information
Furnished By The Chief Engineer. Break Down Design Into Workable
Units And Prepare Preliminary Design Layouts And Production Drawings.
Check All Information On Components, Parts And Assemblies Under Study
Using Graphs, Calculations, Etc., To Clarify Design. Perform Projects
In Areas Such As: Structural, Load Path, Clearance, Interference And
Fits On Complicated Mechanisms, Etc. Acted As Lead Man, Supervising
4 To 5 Draftsmen.

The next résumé (7) is too short. You don't know enough about the man after you've finished reading his résumé. You don't know how successful he was on the job. Knowing the companies he worked for and his job titles is simply not enough. In contrast, Résumé 8 is complete but not excessive. It sells experience and accomplishments in a business-like fashion.

The amazing thing is this: Résumé 8 was written by the same

RÉSUMÉ 7.

HOWARD S. SMITH
25 Colfax Road
Manasquan, New Jersey
(201) 722-6709

SUPERMARKET & MASS MARKETING SALES EXPERIENCE

Field Sales Broker	Barker Associates	1/66 to Present
Nat'l Mgr. Supers	Treadwell Co.	4/62 to 1/66
Sales Mgr. Supers	May & Hamilton	8/59 to 4/62
Regional Mgr.	Sells-Warfield	1/54 to 8/59
District Mgr.	Wilson Prod. Corp.	4/50 to 1/54
Salesman	Hill & Lawn	6/48 to 4/50

RESUME

Currently operating as a Field Broker for manufacturers specializing in selling to supermarkets and mass marketers through a network of food brokers and sales representatives. During this period I have worked with Lindon Industries, Marmite Towels, ABC Plastics, Martin Shampoos, A J. Thompson, Inc., Lawrenceville Toiletries and others. I have managed the brokers in the field, set up quotas and incentive plans, devised catalog and selling sheets, and acted as sales manager for most of these companies.

With Hill & Lawn completely set up network of Brokers for the supermarket trade and directed these brokers through regional managers.

EDUCATION

Univ. of Washington	Psychology		1940 - 1943
Columbia Univ.	Law	A.B.	1946 - 1947
N.Y.C. (nights)	Marketing		1948 - 1950

PERSONAL DATA

Born Jan. 15, 1928   Health - excellent   5'10"   185 lbs.

Married with two children

MILITARY

Army - May '43 to June '46 - Captain

REFERENCES

Available on request and from every previous employer

man who wrote Résumé 6. The difference is simply that when the author rewrote his résumé he focussed on a quick statement of responsibility, followed by a record of results.

RÉSUMÉ 8.

Ralph Carstair   Married
143 Apple Valley Road   Two Dependents
Seattle, Washington   Height 5'8"   Weight 165
(206)   778-6391   Health - Excellent

OBJECTIVE: Mechanical, Structural Engineer in a position which
                    affords opportunity for creative engineering
                    innovation

MILITARY AND
COMMERCIAL
ENGINEERING
EXPERIENCE: BATTLESON AIRCRAFT COMPANY, Seattle, Washington

1969-1970   Mechanical Design Engineer   Duties included layout
                    of highly sophisticated major assembly jigs.

                    Although at Battleson only nine months, was able to
                    replace a variety of transportation dollies with a
                    single "multiuse" type transportation dolly system.
                    New system saved needed production space and
                    investment in dollies.

1964-1969   ASTRO GENERAL AIRCRAFT CORPORATION, Los Angeles,
                    California.

                    Structural Design Engineer   Duties included
                    preliminary-through-production design of aerospace
                    components.

                    Developed method of adapting the ejection seat
                    escape system from the Apollo "A" program to meet
                    the requirements of "B" program.   Acted as lead
                    engineer for this activity.

                    Requested by management to participate in critical
                    design review meeting of the Apollo "B" program held
                    within the government.

                    As a result of contributions to Apollo program, was
                    selected to be part of advance design group for the
                    manned space laboratory system study, which led to
                    an invitation to work directly with NASA officials
                    in Washington, D.C.

1957-1964   ROBINSON-DAVIS CORPORATION, St. Louis, Missouri

                   Development Engineer   Duties included design and
                   development of guided missile components.

                   Created a new dimensioning system to standardize
                   five different individual systems previously in
                   use in the plant. New system simplified design
                   communications, improved tolerance of component
                   parts and resulted in increased productivity.

                   As a result of dimensioning system acceptance, was
                   promoted to Design Group Leader, responsible for
                   activities of four-man practical engineering group.

                   Started as Design Draftsman (1957), promoted to
                   Mechanical Designer (1958-1961) and then advanced to
                   Development Engineer (1961-1964).

                   Approved for appointment to Materials Review Board
                   by Robinson-Davis Corporation, Air-Davis Aircraft
                   Company and U.S. Government Agency.

1955-1957   FARR-CHAMBERS CORPORATION, Hamilton Signal Division,
                   Kansas City, Kansas

                   Design Engineer   Duties included layout and design
                   of multiengine bi-track vehicles. Developed a
                   power train that allowed use of standard automotive
                   production engines. This provided easy transfer to
                   wartime production without costly delays and
                   retooling.

1954-1955   DYNO-SCAN CORPORATION, Outboard Engine Division,
                   Kansas City, Kansas

                   Project Engineer   Responsible for first 50 h.p.
                   outboard motor manufactured and sold by Dyno-scan
                   Corporation from concept through final engineering.

                   Responsible for twenty-man design team that devel-
                   oped this engine. This item was successfully
                   introduced and marketed by R, S, & P. Stores. One
                   engineering feature, basic to the marketing success
                   of this engine, was a fuel pump lower than that
                   found in leading outboards, which allowed for more
                   streamlined silhouette and styling.

1948-1954   COURAGE MANUFACTURING COMPANY, Kansas City, Missouri

                   DUNSTON CORPORATION, Aeronautics Division,
                   Kansas City, Missouri

1948 - 1954   MANNFIELD MANUFACTURING COMPANY, East Moline, Kansas
(continued)
                   BROWN MOTOR COMPANY, East Moline, Kansas

                   My first six years in business were spent with the
                   above companies creating a wide base of development
                   and design experience.

                   As part of a two-man engineering staff, recommended
                   changes in production flow which were accepted by
                   Courage Products management and put into effect.

                   Designed one of the first jet-spray sprinklers
                   marketed in 1951, several years before this type of
                   sprinkler became popular.

EDUCATION:

1961-1963   HAWTHORNE COLLEGE, Akron, Ohio

                   Majored in Mechanical Engineering Technology.
                   Worked nights to support family.

1946 - 1948   CENTRAL MICHIGAN TECHNICAL COLLEGE, Birmingham,
                   Michigan

                   Full-time student - majored in Engineering Technology.
                   On tennis team. Founded undergraduate Engineering
                   Society.

                   Certified as Senior Engineering Technician by
                   The Institute of Engineering Technicians,
                   Washington, D.C.

MILITARY
SERVICE:

1944 - 1946   Honorable Discharge, U.S. Army, World War II.
                   Sergeant.

PERSONAL
BACKGROUND: Grew up in Shaker Heights, Ohio, and attended Shaker
                   Heights public schools. Hobbies include photography
                   and painting. Am an old movie buff. Have been an
                   ardent tennis player for many years.

REFERENCES: References will be forwarded on request.

● The difference between too long or too short a résumé and
the one which is complete and readable is usually a matter of
editing. The task ahead of you is to write everything down that

you feel should be in your résumé, and then cut it down to a point where you know there is not a single superfluous word. It's not easy, but it can be done. The Rolls-Royce ads by David Ogilvy were 700 words each, but you won't find a single wasted word in one of them. Say the same for your résumé.

• Relate your accomplishments to a specific time and place. Résumé 9 sells its author's accomplishments, but it is difficult to relate them to a real time and place. Hence, you are less likely to be convinced by them. Résumé 8 was just the opposite. You know precisely when and for whom the man's accomplishments were made. Put your accomplishments right after each of the jobs you held, so that your prospective boss knows they are real, tangible contributions, not made up for your résumé. The résumé that sells generalized accomplishments reminds me of the ad for the headache remedy that promised "50 per cent faster pain relief." Every time I see that ad, I ask myself, "Than what?"

• Include a job objective at the beginning of your résumé. This job objective should be as specific as you can make it as to the kind of job you want to have. (Review Résumés 2, 4, and 8.) Now, it may well be that your job objective eliminates you from interviews with companies which are not seeking a man with the job objective you state. So be it. If the company doesn't want or isn't looking for a man with a job objective like your own, why waste your time interviewing them in the first place? There is nothing more frustrating than going through a series of interviews with a company for which you would like to work, only to find out in the end that the job opening is of no interest to you. So, while a specific job objective may limit your interviews, it should ultimately save you valuable time.

When I suggest to job-seekers that they include a specific job objective at the start of their résumés, I am often confronted with the following question, "Suppose there are two jobs I'd be equally happy with? What should I do then?" Before I suggest what to do, let me tell you what not to do. Don't put both objec-

RÉSUMÉ 9.

ALLEN FORESTER
137 Harvard Avenue
Old Greenwich, Connecticut

E D U C A T I O N   1952 B.A.   Industrial Management,
Stevens Institute of Technology
1957-1959   Industrial Pharmaceutical Mfg.,
eight graduate hours,
Fordham University School of Pharmacy
1959-1961   Industrial Engineering,
Monmouth University Engineering College

P R O F E S S I O N A L B A C K G R O U N D

Administration
Administered and coordinated plant operations involving
manufacturing, packaging, personnel training, equipment selection,
cost reduction, plant layouts, facilities planning.

Manufacturing
Experience in metalworking operations, pharmaceutical tablet,
liquid, ointment, sterile products, disposable hospital supplies,
intravenous devices, electronic manufacturing.

Packaging
Designed, installed high speed automatic, semi-automatic packaging
lines, manual, bench, conveyor, inspection, strip packaging,
blister, sample operations.

Cost Systems, Budget Controls, Profit and Loss
Established manufacturing operating costs, manpower utilization,
standard cost system, labor estimates, profit and loss analysis,
cost performance to budgets.

Method Improvement - Inventory Control
Organized methods and procedures improving manufacturing, clerical
operations, inventory control operations.

Marketing - Package Development
Coordinated activities of marketing, package development with
manufacturing. Recommended packages for machinery, material and
labor economy.

Facilities Planning - Warehousing - Material Handling
Planned, designed new manufacturing and warehouse facilities, order
picking, packing, shipping. Materials handling bulk finished goods.
Physical distribution studies.

E M P L O Y M E N T H I S T O R Y

1968 to 1970   Assistant to Director of Manufacturing
Astrogen Corporation, Consumer Products Division,
New York City

56

1956 to 1968	Manager, Plant Engineering
	Grover Company, Fort Lee, New Jersey
1948 to 1956	Group Head - Industrial Engineering
	Datatronics Corporation, Fort Lee, New Jersey
1945 to 1948	Senior Industrial Engineer
	Undertown Corporation, Princeton, New Jersey
1942 to 1945	U.S. Navy

A F F I L I A T I O N S

Association of Professional Engineers, Senior Member
Packing Institute, Senior Engineering Associate
Licensed Professional Engineer

P E R S O N A L   Born, April 28, 1924, Married, Two Children

tives on the same résumé. Don't suggest to your prospective employer that you'd be equally happy as a staff adviser for manufacturing or as a line production manager.

In the first place, that little word "or" suggests that you are not particularly single-minded. It's a great word to leave out of a résumé. In the second place, the word "or" makes you look a little too flexible. Putting it more bluntly, when you include the word "or," it appears that you can't make up your own mind. At this point you may get angry enough to say, "O.K. then, you suggest that I don't put both objectives on the same résumé. Then what do I do?" The answer is obvious. Prepare two résumés. Send one to one kind of company, the second to the other kind of company. Or, if you have a preferred objective, send the first résumé to all companies. But if an employment agency or executive recruiter calls you and indicates a job in the area of your secondary interest is available, you still have a résumé on tap to send for that specific job opportunity.

If you don't have a preferred job objective and several areas appeal equally to you, let me offer the following course of action. Include in your job objective specific elements common to each of the several alternative positions that interest you. To illustrate this approach, consider the man who worked first for an advertising agency as an account executive and later for a company as an advertising manager. He felt the need to move on, and was willing to work on either side of the fence. What did his job objective look like?

> A position as an advertising administrator, dealing with the supervision of advertising budgets, the establishment of advertising strategies, and the evaluation of copy and media performance.

The kind of job he sought existed at either the advertising agency or a company. Thus, his objective fitted both his alternatives and was still specific enough to be of interest to the prospective bosses at an agency or company.

Whatever you do, don't take the easy way out and leave off your job objective. In the first place it is now fairly standard to include a job objective. If you leave it off, you look like a man who doesn't know where he wants to go. That's bad. Second, every great ad asks in some way for the order. Your job objective is your way of asking for the job you want. It's your opportunity to stretch a little, to seek out a better job than you now have. And you can be sure, if you don't go after the better and bigger job, it certainly isn't going to find its way to you. Your job objective, then, is your single biggest opportunity to move up the ladder when you make a company change. Don't overlook it.

3 / How to be liked without being known . . . how good does your résumé look?   Like it or not, your résumé is in the hands of your prospective boss long before you have a chance to sell yourself in person. Since you're not there to defend it, your résumé must turn on your prospective boss, or you'll never get a chance to do so personally. When you consider that your résumé is *prima facie* evidence of your writing ability, your organizational ability, and your approach to business problems, it's amazing how many résumés look as if they were literally thrown together. Just for a moment, then, let's pretend you're a personnel director and together let's look at some real-life résumés to determine what kind of men wrote them. For the moment, disregard the contents. Let's evaluate the men based solely on the appearance of their résumés.

● The overlong résumé. Winston Churchill was once complimented on a speech that lasted one hour. He was asked how long it took to write it. He replied that it took two hours to write that particular speech. "Amazing," the interviewer interjected. "Not really," said Sir Winston. "I could have written a half-hour speech if I'd had four hours to write it." If you are long-winded in your résumé, chances are you'll be long-winded at the weekly executive committee meeting. (And you probably won't get that chance.) Unless your career is exceptional, two pages should suffice—at the outside, three pages. Résumés as long as five and six pages are a bore. Chances are your prospective boss won't read beyond page two or three but will throw down your résumé in disgust and move on to the next one.

● The overdetailed résumé. One reason résumés sometimes get too long is because they are too detailed. Consider the first page of Résumé 10. The writer suffers from verbosity. He fails to isolate the significance of his background. He includes excess verbiage because he doesn't have the time or skills required to isolate the important things in his career. A résumé that is overdetailed is, in point of fact, insulting because it assumes the prospective boss who read it has little or no understanding of the scope of the job he is seeking to fill. If you are applying for a job as a plant manager, you shouldn't need to describe every piece of equipment that you've ever dealt with. It's the scope of your operation that is going to be evaluated: how many people you worked with, what kind of industries the plants you managed were in. In a word, give your prospective boss credit for being able to realize the details of your current operation and sell him on the breadth of your experience.

What kind of men wrote these overdetailed résumés? As a prospective employer you might well assume that the men are involved with minutiae, probably unable to communicate broad,

RÉSUMÉ 10.

EDWARD J. LOWENSTEIN

1449-71 Mosholu Parkway
Brooklyn, N.Y.   10443
(212) UL-9-4172

OBJECTIVE

To hold a position of responsibility commensurate with my experience
where I can successfully guide people and give direction to the
profitable manufacturing of products.

1968 to present

Director of Manufacturing of a medium-sized company engaged in
the manufacture of dermatological products, ethical and proprietary.
My job is to schedule production dependent upon the needs of quarterly
supply. I am responsible too for all purchasing from raw materials to
finished product. I coordinate all purchasing with production requirements, keeping a reasonably smooth flow of material into the plant and
no back orders. (When I first arrived at this company, the back order
collection on some items was six months.)

Because my machinery experience is so extensive, it is my duty to
decide on the purchase of new equipment to suit the special needs of
these very special formulas.

For the first time in the history of the company, because of the
employment of my production techniques, the company has assay proof products. (All products sampled at any point in production pass inspection
based on label requirements.)

In addition the fill requirements for tube, bottle or jar are
exactly as required. This is important particularly in bottle fill production. Some formulas are very light and full of air and consequently
the bottles are passed through without being entirely filled. To offset
this some firms use larger bottles (in length and diameter)... this
means changing problems all the way down the packaging line, such as
boxes, etc. The company used to rework the ingredients (heat to fluidity,
etc. so as to be able to fill into bottles.) This is no longer a problem.
They can now take stored material at room temperature and fill without
reworking.

The company's most valued product ingredient used to be troublesome.
A precipitate would develop in whatever product it was incorporated...
such as hair tonics and suntan lotions. Using the method I introduced,
the precipitate is removed from the distillate fraction before it is
stored for incorporating into the various products. I might add that
filtration did not work. At first it appears to be sufficient, but
after a week of standing it becomes obvious that the material is so fine
it passes through even the finest of filters. (Experiments proved.)

These accomplishments, in addition to the daily routine of assigning
job work to the people are a sample of the nature of the way I work.

basic generalizations. When you prepare your own résumé,
make sure your background and accomplishments are simple
and broad-brush. Don't be thought of as thinking small, or you
may never have the opportunity to think big.

1964-1968   MANON FRERES
             605 Fifth Avenue
             New York, N.Y.

Manufacturing Manager in charge of all private label production.
Products ranged widely, including essential oils to finished body treat-
ment items. I had complete charge of all phases of production including
purchasing of new equipment, raw materials, packaging materials (where
needed), planning, personnel supervision, and coordination between the
lab, marketing, and production.

1956-1963   ROSE DAWSON LTD.
             New Brunswick, N.J.

President and general manager but did not own any stock. Responsible for all phases of the physical operation -- not responsible for sales
or financing.
Rose Dawson is a firm engaged in the manufacture of dry skin cosmetics and most famous for the unique fragrance of its dry scalp conditioner.
When I joined the company, they were doing about $600,000 to $700,000
in net billing. When I left, they were in the neighborhood of $16,000,000
per year in net billing. I like to think that I was in large part responsible for keeping pace with this phenomenal growth by attending to all
duties other than the two described above which were in other competent
hands.
Duties included production, research and development, purchasing,
personnel, package design, and development of equipment to handle
packaging needs from bulk to high-speed separation into multi-sized
containers.

● The slipshod résumé. The number of unprofessional
résumés sent out by job-seekers would astound you. The variety
of goofs would make you cringe. For the record, here are some
of the more common faults that could turn off your readers before they get started:

1. Overcrowded pages with next-to-no margins—looks as if
   the author was too cheap to run off a second page.
2. Difficult-to-read copies that were undoubtedly duplicated
   in the back office for nothing—and are worth about that
   much.
3. Typographical errors that glare off the page.
4. Paragraphs and words that don't line up—the probable result of home typing on a beat-up college portable, or past-

ing and clipping last year's résumé to this year's update. If you look carefully at the first page of the next résumé you'll note that the last paragraph doesn't have the same type face as the ones above it. And also that the sequence of jobs is out of order. Quite obviously the author used the space at the bottom of his last résumé to type in his most recent experience. Not quite the professional you'd hire to be your next chief engineer (Résumé 11).

5. Blurred letters (you wish you had some fluid to clean the keys).

6. Changes in format, spelling, and style between the first paragraphs and last.

In words of one syllable, the men who send such résumés are slobs. Would you want a slob working for you? Do you think your prospective boss wants a slob working for him? The answer is "no" to both questions. For God's sake, then, don't be cheap with your time or money when it comes to making your résumé look good. Make sure it's typed professionally with plenty of white space so the elements in your résumé show up. Check for typographical errors. This may be more difficult than you think. If you have your résumé typed by a résumé service, they'll expect you to approve the master sheet at a moment's notice after it has been typed. Lose a day. Take the master home with you. Check it thoroughly. There's nothing more amateurish than a résumé with typos in it. It reminds me of the young man who wrote to the college of his choice and asked if they would "except" him. You can bet your bottom dollar they most assuredly did. In short, don't run the risk of looking unprofessional. If your résumé is, your prospective boss will certainly think you are.

• The buried treasure résumé. In recent years a number of résumé counselors have suggested that accomplishments be included in résumés. Unfortunately, for one reason or another, these counselors haven't made any firm recommendation as to

RÉSUMÉ 11.

RESUME OF RECENT EXPERIENCE

ASSOCIATE
PROFESSOR

September 1966 to July 1968   Trenton Engineering College
Trenton, New Jersey

Taught Architectural Drafting - Second year.
Introduction to architectural drafting, Space design,
Room & House design, Floor plans, Elevations, perspective
& rendering, Roof & House frame structure design, New
Jersey building codes.

Taught Mechanical Drafting - First, Second & Third year.
Basic mechanical drafting, Orthographics, Sketching,
Introduction to descriptive geometry and geometric
projection, Introduction to Technical Illustration &
Industrial design, Solving industrial problems of design.

September 1964 to July 1966

Purdue University
Lafayette, Indiana

ASSISTANT
PROFESSOR

Designed two year terminal course and taught various
aspects of vocational drafting for engineering technician
related to design and manufacture of electro-mechanical
products.

Mathematics: trigonometry, vector forces - two and three
dimensional force systems, Quality control: specifications
and engineering drawing interpretation for manufacture and
quality control, tooling, holding and clamping devices,
Introduction to fluidic science, Manufacturing processes,
Geometric and positional tolerances, Basic and advanced
Mechanical drafting, instrument drawings, A Study of
production problems. Introduced a new seminar, Concept of
Dimensions, which studies spatial perception.

July 1968 to October 1971   Galaxie Industries
Trenton, N.J.

SENIOR
ENGINEER

In charge of engineering and production. Established
Management Committee, procedures manual, inventory and
purchasing controls. Set up quality control program.
Established an engineering committee. Started time study
data collection to establish standards. Increased
production by initiating supervisory training program in
time & motion study.

how to include accomplishments in the résumé itself. Thus, all
too often I read résumés with accomplishments literally
squeezed in at the ends of paragraphs, hidden from all but the
most persevering reader (Résumé 12). Because few prospective

RÉSUMÉ 12.

MARTIN SPRINGER
14701 Town Line Road
Cleveland Heights, Ohio
216-932-4808

― ―

PERSONAL DATA:

Age: 47. Married. Two children. Am an ardent tennis player.
Active in community affairs. Enjoy hunting and fishing.

― ―

MILITARY SERVICE:

In Army for two years during World War II. Attended Princeton University
and Williams College for three months each for West Point Preparatory
Courses. Honorably discharged.

― ―

EDUCATION:

Attended Kenyon College for two years. Attended Ohio State University for
one year. Majored in business administration.

― ―

EMPLOYMENT HISTORY:

I. 1968 to Present
    AVONDALE REALTY COMPANY, Cleveland, Ohio
    Vice President and Director. Responsible for development of sales
    promotion programs, placement of advertising in local newspapers,
    securing photographs of property listed by Avondale, including aerial
    photography of industrial sites. Responsible for liaison between
    mortgage companies and legal firms representing buyer and seller.
    Negotiate with buyers and sellers to determine final sale price.
    Responsible for keeping records of all transactions made on weekly and
    monthly basis, and for administration of office personnel. Sold over
    4 million dollars in 18 months to increase company sales versus
    previous year by 15 per cent.

II. 1964 to 1968
    AVONDALE REALTY COMPANY, a division of AVONDALE CORPORATION.
    Vice President and General Manager. Director of Residential Marketing.
    Until spin-off in 1968, Avondale Realty was part of Avondale Land
    Development Corporation. Was responsible for administration of office
    personnel, development of advertising campaigns, and placement of ads
    in newspapers. Developed long and short range plans for corporation
    growth. Sold condominium property. Responsible for Avondale
    Information Center operation. Responsible for analyzing results of 25
    sales people and training to improve performance. Created concept of
    "Information Center," which has been credited with doubling Avondale
    residential property sales, now standard industry practice.

bosses will persevere, it will pay you to separate your accomplishments from your brief job description so that both stand out, as the same writer has done in this revised version of his résumé (13).

RÉSUMÉ 13.

MARTIN SPRINGER   Married
14701 Town Line Road   3 Dependents
Cleveland Heights, Ohio   170 lbs. 5'10"
216-932-4808   Health: Excellent

JOB   Senior real estate marketing management position
OBJECTIVE: with dynamic company.

REAL ESTATE
MARKETING   AVONDALE REALTY COMPANY
EXPERIENCE: Cleveland, Ohio

January 1968   Vice President and Director
- Present
                  Responsible for overall management of company in
                  owner's absence and creation of all sales and
                  marketing programs.

                  Personally sold over four million dollars in
                  investment real estate in 18 months, to increase
                  total company sales by 15% over previous year.

                  Joined Avondale Realty at request of new owner,
                  following spin-off from Avondale Corporation.

June 1964 -   AVONDALE REALTY COMPANY
January 1968   a division of AVONDALE CORPORATION

                  Vice President and General Manager
                  - Avondale Realty Company
                  Director of Residential Marketing
                  - Avondale Corporation

                  Responsible for management of realty company
                  including finance, personnel, advertising, short
                  and long term planning, condominium sales.
                  Developed Avondale Information Center. Responsible
                  for administering and training staff of 25 people.

                  Maintained $40-55,000 net profit each year.
                  Administered full marketing program for Avondale
                  Corporation. Member of Division Management Committee.

                  "Information Center" led to doubling of corporate
                  residential sales, and is now standard industry
                  practice.

                  Industry honors:

                  Elected President of Pierce County Business
                  Development Association 1967-68

                  Recipient of Life Member Million Dollar Circle
                  Award, U.S. Real Estate Association (for four
                  consecutive years of $1 million plus sales).

65

● The make-do résumé. The number of people who have the audacity (or stupidity) to send last year's résumé for this year's job is mind-boggling. This fault is not limited to neophyte job-seekers, either. I have received numerous résumés from senior executives, prepared for a distant time in the past and supplemented with an addendum or overriding letter. My attitude toward these résumés—(and I'm sure the attitude of most prospective employers)—is to question the sincerity of the job-seekers in applying for the position. It costs no more than $10 or $15 to have a résumé updated. If you really mean business, surely it's worth that much to turn out a current sales message about yourself.

Last year's résumé, with addendum attached, is not the only kind of make-do résumé. Another lulu is the résumé written originally to go after a particular job, such as engineer, but sent out in response to ads for a totally different kind of position, such as production supervisor. Frequently its author underlines the one or two relevant paragraphs in the candidate's otherwise nonrelevant background, lest they be overlooked. My attitude, and again the likely attitude of prospective bosses, to such make-do résumés has to be this: If the candidate in question really wanted to be considered seriously, why didn't he rewrite his résumé, stressing his experience, however limited, in the field for which he is now applying for a job. Tidbits, even underlined, are not enough.

● The glamour-puss résumé, prepared by a one-flight-up résumé-writing firm. You can spot this kind of résumé a mile away. It may have a gold or blue border. It may be printed in maroon or green ink. It may use a very bold IBM type face. It may be printed on a stock so stiff it can't be folded. Anything to stand out. And it does—as a résumé that was not written by you. Your prospective boss is interested in what you have done —not anyone else but you. And that includes the ability to organize your career in a meaningful way to him.

4 | It's the little things that count.   About now you are proba-
bly itchy to start writing your own résumé. Your list of significant contributions has been long completed, and you know how
format and appearance make the difference between a résumé
that sells hard and one that doesn't sell at all. Before you start
writing your résumé, however, there are a few more ideas (small
points, perhaps) that might prove valuable to know.

• Don't lie—not even a "white" lie. This sounds quite simple.
But you'd be surprised at how many alter the past, particularly
if they feel it is detrimental to them. White lies invariably come
back to haunt. Why take the chance? One small case history
should, I think, prove to you the value of being totally honest.
An eager young executive, about thirty, whom I counseled a few
years ago related this incident to me.

When he was twenty-three, the young executive secured a job
that, shortly after accepting it, he found totally unsatisfactory
for many reasons. He hated his boss. The work bored him to
tears. And, not surprisingly, his boss didn't think much of him.
The executive quit in disgust after only four months. (He decided to resign before he got fired.) Thinking any reference to
this sad four months to be awkward, he decided to amend his
past on a résumé he wrote several years later. Thus, he left out
this unhappy four months of his life and instead stated that his
next job had started four months earlier than it actually had.
The young executive figured no one would know the difference.
In the back of his mind, he felt this little lie would avoid the
possibility of someone calling the company where he had toiled
sadly for only four months, and where he felt his reputation
could be tarnished. As you might expect, in true tales of this
sort, it just so happened that the personnel director at the very
company the young executive was most interested in decided to
check past history. In the search, the first thing the personnel
director turned up was that the stated dates of employment did
not correspond with the actual dates at the young executive's

previous job. Needless to say, it didn't take much digging to find out about the four-month job that didn't work out well. The young executive was subsequently called in by the personnel director and confronted with the lost four months. He was indeed embarrassed by the situation. As it turned out, another candidate was selected by this company. The young executive who related this story to me felt that his white lie was the deciding factor in his not getting the job he wanted. He was sure he was the most qualified for it.

• Don't attach a photograph. If you're like most men, a girl in a slinky black negligee appears sexier to you than the same girl in her birthday suit. The slinky negligee leaves something mysterious, unknown, and unstated, for your curiosity to dwell on. The same holds true for your résumé. If you give away everything, there's nothing left to tantalize. One thing you can and should hold back is your photograph. If he's interested in your résumé, your prospective boss will be anxious to see what you really look like. Don't make it too easy for him. Don't attach your photograph. You might be less handsome than you think you are.

• Don't state on your résumé your salary objective, nor the salary you are paid on your current job. If there's one thing I've come to realize in my years in business, it's that "salary ranges" are flexible guidelines at best. If a company really wants you, and you're the absolutely right man for the job, there is invariably a way for that company to stretch to meet your needs. Similarly, if a man really wants a job and he believes it offers the potential for a lifetime career, he's likely to bend just a little bit from his own salary requirements.

With these two points in mind, it makes little sense to include your salary objective or current salary in your résumé. Even if your financial demands are rigid, it still is less than wise to include them on your résumé. I think you'll agree with me if you recall for a second that your résumé is truly your personal advertisement. Cadillac and Lincoln ads don't mention the price tag.

They sell the quality of these automobiles. The ads attempt to persuade you to go down to the showroom, where a salesman will review the car's merits in person. The hope is you'll be sufficiently impressed to ante up the seven grand. Your résumé's primary job is to get you into your prospective boss's office, where you'll have a chance to sell yourself in person. Don't frighten your prospective boss off with a résumé that says you're expensive. Unless you're selling your services at discount prices, sell quality, not your price tag.

• Don't name your references. There are several reasons why you ought not to name references in your résumé. In the first place, as with enclosing your photograph, you leave your prospective boss with one less reason for asking you to come to his office, one less opportunity for you to meet with him face to face, where you can sell him on your accomplishments. Second, it's a nuisance to the persons you use as references when you broadcast their names and addresses on every résumé you send out. You'll find your references like it (and you) a whole lot better when they are called on infrequently. So, wait until you're asked for references. Then be prepared to give the names, addresses, and phone numbers of those persons who can say what you want them to say about your past experience.

One more point: Whatever you do, don't include a written "To whom it may concern" reference from a former employer who is wishing you well. In the first place, these form references are typically written in a most perfunctory manner and, as such, are not strong endorsements of you. In the second place, they can't possibly relate to the specific job needs of the prospective boss you are now pursuing. This leads back to the strategy stated above: Wait until you've been requested to give a reference. Then give the name of a former employer or other reference who can answer questions about you in relationship to the job you now want.

• Never leave out a portion of your life. Several years ago I was asked to review a résumé written by a business associate's close personal friend. While looking it over for form and content, the first thing I noticed was that the résumé included no reference whatsoever to higher education. I asked to meet the job-seeker in person. When we got together, I questioned him about his college education. He told me that he had completed only two years of college. He therefore decided to leave off his education entirely, on the theory that the missing section would go unnoticed. Unfortunately, the absence of a portion of your life is always noticed. It doesn't pay to leave it off, since you only create question marks in the interviewer's mind concerning your honesty and candor.

• Include something personal. Given a choice between two men, your prospective boss will have to hire the one who appears to be capable of accomplishing most for him. But, given a situation where you and someone else have similar experience and have made nearly identical contributions, then the swing factor may well be something totally unrelated to business. For example, you and your prospective boss may both play tennis. Your prospective boss may need a fourth, and, just that simply, you may get a job. If you doubt that personal information can sometimes spell the difference between a turndown and an interview, consider this. A manufacturing-staff friend of mine told me about the job interview that led to his current job. It seems he and his interviewer didn't talk business for very long. Somehow or other the conversation turned to a small item at the bottom of his résumé, the small town where my friend had grown up. It turned out to be the same hamlet in western Canada that the prospective boss came from. The common geographic background of the prospective boss and potential employee brought the two together. My manufacturing-staff friend was offered the job and accepted it. Keep in mind, then, that something personal can make a difference. And you can never tell what personal item on your résumé is going to be of greatest interest to your prospective boss. Frequently sports are a common denominator. It might be hobbies such as woodworking or photography. It might just be old school ties, or civic associations in which you are active, such as Lions or Elks. It could even be a political group or church organization.

At this point I am often asked whether or not the mention of political groups or church affiliations can hurt. Suppose your prospective boss is a Republican and you are a Democrat. Will that knock you out of the ball game? With a few bigoted people, yes. But you wouldn't want to work for them anyhow. On the other hand, if you present your personal background in a positive fashion, you're likely to touch upon a common interest that could be beneficial in your interview. For example, you may be in charge of the speakers' program for Kiwanis; your prospective boss may be in charge of the speakers' program for the Junior Chamber of Commerce. He may want to learn more about the speakers' program in your organization. And . . . your résumé may well end up in the stack marked "arrange for interview" instead of that other stack to receive the usual "Dear John" letter.

• Don't think your résumé couldn't be improved. In ten years of counseling job-seekers, I've yet to see a single résumé that couldn't be touched up in one way or another. And that includes my own. Periodically, I return to my résumé. Each time I find a word here or a sentence there that could be changed to make accomplishments stand out more quickly, seem clearer or more cogent. If you'll buy the idea that the first résumé you put together may not be the most brilliant ever written, consider these three suggestions.

1. Let some business friends read over your résumé after it's finished but before the final typing. Ask them to look critically at its format, appearance, and content. Take their criticism to heart. They are your friends.
2. After you have had three or four interviews, look critically

at your résumé again. Ask yourself whether or not during the course of your interviews you talk about accomplishments that are not included on your résumé. Ask yourself if there are any aspects of your résumé that prospective bosses seem to want you to clarify. Revise your résumé based on what you learned from these early interviews. Be sure your résumé sells you on paper as well as you sell yourself in person.

3. Have your résumé rerun if it isn't perfect the first time. If you're thinking about changing jobs, or perhaps you're out of work, the ten dollars it takes to rerun your résumé may seem like a lot of money. But ten bucks is really small potatoes when you compare it to the extra money you'll make if your résumé sells you harder than your competition. Don't be penny wise and pound foolish. If you think you can improve it, rework your résumé. Have it rerun. Don't put a ten-dollar bill in between you and a better job.

5 / *The perfect résumé.* Early in this chapter I suggested that there probably isn't such a thing as an ideal résumé. Nonetheless, I have often been asked to provide a simple-to-follow outline that synopsizes the principles I have developed over a decade of analyzing résumés that do and don't make the grade. As you read the following résumé guide, please don't keep it in your mind as the summa cum laude of résumé outlines. It isn't. It does, however, highlight what you've done, where you're going, and what accomplishments you've achieved along the way.

This reverse-chronological outline is most appropriate to those of you whose careers have been single-minded, since it obviously focuses on your recent accomplishments.

As you read the suggested outline, several things will be apparent to you: There's plenty of white space. Paragraphs are short. Job titles are underlined. Company names are in capital letters. The types of experience you've had are keyed in the left-hand margin, as well as the dates of this experience.

RÉSUMÉ GUIDE

YOUR FULL NAME
Your home address
Your home phone number

Your marital status
Number of dependents
Your height and weight
Your health status

JOB
OBJECTIVE:

State succinctly the type of position you seek. If you have several objectives, make up several resumes. Don't use "or" in your objective. (Who needs a guy who can't make up his mind?)

BUSINESS
EXPERIENCE:

If you've had more than one type of business experience and you wish to focus on that fact, you may divide your experience into parts. For example: Purchasing experience, Manufacturing experience. Use the left-hand margin for this purpose.

Inclusive Dates:
(e.g. 1967—1969)

NAME OF MOST RECENT COMPANY in capital letters, location in upper and lower case (e.g. AUSTIN, KENT & PAYNE, Inc., New York, N.Y.)

Your title presently, or when you left, underlined. (e.g. Advertising Director, Small Appliance Division)

Short one-paragraph description of your responsibilities (maximum: four sentences). Description should emphasize scope of your operation, scope of your management function. Avoid minutiae.

Your prospective employer does not need to be told that among your duties as Advertising Director you maintained files of competitive ads, represented your company at A.N.A. meetings, analyzed competitive media trends. That's all nice. But it's expected of you and so is insignificant. The important facts are the media budget you controlled, the number of agencies with which you worked directly, etc.

Two to three short, pithy paragraphs (each no more than three sentences) describing your accomplishments. Make the "results" statements come across fast and dramatically. Don't bury your accomplishments. No one has time for digging. Include industry honors, recognition, if any.

Inclusive Dates:
Previous Position
(e.g. 1962–1967)

NAME OF PREVIOUS COMPANY AFFILIATION, location.

Your title on leaving.

Short paragraphs outlining responsibilities and accomplishments, as indicated above. Your description of this previous job should be shorter than that of your current (or last) job since your most recent experience is more relevant than previous experience.

If you have worked at the same company in several, progressively more responsible positions, you should highlight this fact by citing titles and accomplishments chronologically with most recent title first. State dates you have held each title.

(e.g. 1968–1969
     1967–1968
     1966–1967)

e.g.: Advertising Director
      Associate Advertising Director
      Media Coordinator

Be sure you write a description of your job responsibilities and your accomplishments while you held each position.

EDUCATION:

NAME OF LAST SCHOOL ATTENDED, location. (e.g.: PARSONS SCHOOL OF DESIGN, New York, N.Y.)

Inclusive Dates:
(e.g. 1951–1955)

Degree received. Departmental major. One other significant course taken. Honors received. Academic and extracurricular awards. Significant associations in which you held memberships. Offices held, if any. Scholarships received.

Inclusive Dates:
(e.g. 1949–1951)

NAME OF SCHOOL PREVIOUSLY ATTENDED, location.

Use separate paragraph for each college-level or higher academic institution you attended. Do not include paragraph on your high school unless this is your highest educational level. Focus on what's significant. Include "industry seminars" if relevant. Group them together under title: "Continuing Education."

MILITARY SERVICE:

Inclusive Dates: (e.g. 1955–1957)

Indicate rank at discharge, or current rank if still active; branch of service; commendations; medals; promotions, if significant; current draft status. Do not dwell on this experience unless it's a major part of your life. Civilian business experience and education are much more relevant to prospective employers.

SUMMER JOBS:

Include in resume only if genuinely relevant. What you did for two months during college is usually obscure several years later. If you do include summer experience, incorporate it into your "education" paragraphs where chronologically appropriate.

PERSONAL BACKGROUND, CURRENT HOBBIES, INTERESTS, ASSOCIATIONS:

This is your chance to share something in common with your prospective boss—something that can make you stand out from the other candidates with the same qualifications. Use this section to your best advantage. Include your home town, your current hobbies—particularly sports. Include nonbusiness associations in which you are active.

REFERENCES:

Use the following statement: "References will be forwarded on request." Don't give everybody all your references. Some may be better than others for a particular job. Moreover, if your "references" are besieged by requests, they may sour on you.

SALARY OBJECTIVE:

You are not required to include this on a resume and it is strongly recommended that you do not. If you still feel compelled to include it, state "Open." No more.

AGE/RELIGION/ RACE/SEX BIRTHPLACE:

Do not include these items. They are not required and in most states it is illegal to require them.

DATE OF RESUME

6 / Other resume forms.   If your career has been a meandering
affair, and you intend to backtrack—that is, to seek a position
in a field you were in several years ago—you would do well

RÉSUMÉ 14.

PETER VESPANO
31 Point O'Lark Road   Married, 2 children
Plandome, Long Island   6'1", 180 pounds
516-MA-7-2331   Health: excellent

JOB   Senior engineering position with administrative
OBJECTIVE: responsibility for department in fast-moving growth
                        company.

ENGINEERING   Methods Improvement - Inventory Controls
EXPERIENCE AND
CONTRIBUTIONS: Headed department responsible for methods and
                        procedures improvement for manufacturing and support
                        operations, including warehouse inventory control.

                        Devised computerized raw materials inventory flow
                        system tied to delivery times of key suppliers. Was
                        able to reduce raw materials inventory by 20 per cent
                        and increase warehouse ability to meet production
                        needs. As a result, planned warehouse addition was
                        unnecessary.

                        Marketing - Package Coordination

                        Coordinated activities of marketing and package
                        engineering with manufacturing production staff. Was
                        responsible for recommending packages for machinery,
                        material and labor efficiency, as well as new
                        machinery costing and recommendations.

                        Recommended first installation of blow-mold machinery
                        in plant. By making rather than buying our own
                        plastic containers, we saved more than $580,000
                        annually in freight and packaging materials costs.

                        Manufacturing Planning - Warehousing -
                        Material Handling

                        Was responsible for six years of design of new
                        production and warehouse facilities, distribution and
                        shipping centers. Materials handling of bulk finished
                        goods.

                        Engineered completely new conveyor system for automatic

processing of finished goods inventories at two new warehousing centers. New system cut down processing time by approximately 30 per cent and reduced labor by half in each location.

ADMINISTRATIVE
AND STAFF
EXPERIENCE AND
CONTRIBUTIONS:

Administration

Administer and coordinate plant operations involving all departments; production, package engineering, personnel training, equipment selection, financial and facilities planning.

Initiated weekly problem-solving meetings to reduce independent and conflicting department activity. This resulted in far less inter-department friction and improved senior management morale.

Cost Systems - Budget Controls - Profit/Loss

Recommended to departments changes in operational formats, manpower utilization, cost systems profit analysis.

Developed standard cost system that permits incremental value to be determined between departments which creates a more accurate picture of loss when production is scrapped at each stage of manufacture.

EMPLOYMENT
HISTORY:

1969-Present   **Assistant to Vice President
                - Manufacturing**
                PAULEY PHARMACEUTICALS
                Hempstead, New York

1966-1969   **Manager, Industrial Engineering**
                WEBSTER-LAWSON PHARMACEUTICALS DIVISION
                Long Island City, New York

1963-1966   **Group Leader - Industrial Engineer**
                ATLANTIC PLASTICS CORPORATION
                New York, New York

1956-1963   **Senior Industrial Engineer**
                PARTRIDGE-ALLEN, INCORPORATED
                Bronx, New York

EDUCATION:

1961-1962   FORDHAM UNIVERSITY
                Graduate School of Engineering
                Twelve graduate hours toward Masters
                degree.

1956-1958   ST. JOHN'S UNIVERSITY
                School of Pharmacy
                Ten graduate hours. Top grades.

	1951-1954	LONG ISLAND UNIVERSITY Bachelor of Arts degree. Majored in Industrial Management. Member Undergraduate Industrial Engineering Society. Class Representative - Student Council. Basketball Team.
AFFILIATIONS:		American Institute of Industrial Engineers Packaging Institute, Professional Member Licensed Professional Engineer
MILITARY:		Honorable discharge as First Lieutenant, U.S. Army. Served as battalion liaison officer for Inspector General
PERSONAL:		Grew up in Plandome, Long Island. Attended public schools there. Personal interests include hunting, fishing, and boating. Member Manhasset Bay Yacht Club. Have sailed in several competitive regattas.

August, 1971

to consider a résumé outline which focuses first an accomplishments in those areas related to the position you now seek. As indicated earlier, out-of-context accomplishments are not as believable or meaningful as those presented in the context of a specific job at a specific tíme. Nonetheless, you might do well to consider a résumé outline which starts with a list of relevant accomplishments without regard for time or place. Why? Because the reverse-chronological outline would result in burying your earlier (and presumably most relevant) contributions. As the lesser of two evils, state the accomplishments you want remembered up front. Follow up with a list of companies and job descriptions. Résumé 14 provides an excellent example of this format.

One other résumé form you might consider is the letter résumé. It's addressed to the prospective boss and is in sentence rather than telegraphic form. Such a personal type of approach is

FRANCOIS DuVILLION
Apt. 14G Eastcliff Towers
4700 Van Schuyler Avenue
Philadelphia, Pennsylvania   06170

Mr. J. Albrecht
Vice President
Westwood-Lander Corporation
670 Hinsdale Avenue
Chicago, Illinois 60617

Dear Mr. Albrecht:

Recently you placed an advertisement seeking senior Manufacturing
Operations executives. This letter responds to your ad.
Specifically I am seeking a staff manufacturing position which
involves administrative coordination of technical activities,
evaluation of market and acquisition opportunities, and assessment
of manufacturing and financial controls on an ongoing basis.

In evaluating your current manufacturing operations opportunity,
you will be interested in the resume of my background which
follows:

1970 to Present: AMSTAR SERVION, INC., Philadelphia, Pennsylvania

As a Senior Engineering Associate for this consulting firm, manage
projects in component handling, automation, equipment planning
and purchase, plant layout and planning. Involved in merger
assessment.
    Highlight: Devised new product development, manufacturing
and marketing techniques for Ohio wood finishes manufacturer
which resulted in expansion of sales from $60,000 to $750,000
annually. Basis for growth was distribution through distributors
and retail outlets in addition to institutional buyers.

1968-1970: U.S. FOODS, INC., Snack Division, Morris, New Jersey

As Senior Engineer, directed four million dollar snack plant
expansion program. Responsible for development of new procedures,
controls, systems to optimize machinery and manpower, return on
investment in new plant expansion.
    Highlight: Recommended purchase of $500,000 in new cracker-
producing equipment in preference to reconditioning existing
equipment. Management adopted recommendation based on return on
investment of 17 per cent, and study which showed incremental
manufacturing cost equalled equipment cost in two years.

1966-1968: HEALTH AIDS INTERNATIONAL, Clifton, New Jersey

As Senior Industrial Engineer, assessed, improved existing machinery, and recommended new packaging equipment. Helped establish purchasing, production, inventory control systems. Consulted for line management production problems.

Highlight: Recommended purchase of changeover gears for 17 items run on high-speed auto-fill line. Gears shortened changeover time by 35 per cent. Reduced adjustment time after changeover substantially.

1965-1966: NUCLOTHES CLEANER SYSTEMS, Patterson, New Jersey

As Director of Manufacturing, set up production and servicing of coin-op self-service dry-cleaning machines.

1962-1966: PORTERFIELD PRODUCTS COMPANY, Fairlawn, New Jersey

As Project Engineer, was responsible for all planning, technical, and management activities from product development through production on a million-dollar program designed to get Porterfield into production and marketing of disposable food service containers for institutional use. Responsible for purchase of equipment, development of manufacturing systems and financial controls, staffing and training of personnel.

Highlight: Saved 22 per cent on total building costs by utilizing modular construction in development of portable bacteria-free production area. Modular construction saved 50 per cent on moving costs, reduced taxes, and had shorter depreciation period.

1958-1962: Part-Time Employment in Sales and Finance while attending school

For Coleridge Metals Company, visited company's marketing areas and analyzed sales and market information. Based on analyses, developed advertising program resulting in 41 per cent increased sales during campaign.

1954-1957: REMY-ASTRA S.A., Paix Dijon, France

Worked in Control department. Participated in planning for government contract.

In addition to the business experience, you will be interested in my formal education, my professional associations, and personal profile:

1962: Master of Science, NEWARK INSTITUTE OF TECHNOLOGY, Newark, New Jersey

Majored in industrial management and economics. Courses included all phases of business management including cost

accounting, purchasing, marketing, labor and management relations
and business law.

<u>1954:</u> Bachelor of Science, ST. MARY'S COLLEGE, Paix Dijon, France
    Majored in industrial engineering. Was President of
dormitory.

<u>Professional Organizations</u>
    Vice President, Institute of Industrial Engineers, Northern
New Jersey branch; member, A.M.A.

<u>Personal Profile</u>
    U.S. citizen. Speak French, Spanish, English. Lived in
England, France and Switzerland. Am single. Health excellent.

Thank you for reviewing my professional accomplishments and
background. I look forward to meeting with you personally to
review your career opportunity, and my potential contributions to
your firm.

Your sincerely,

Francois DuVillian

Francois DuVillion

(201) 449-1231

used infrequently, and has the merits of being unusual and
warmer in style than the standard format. However, as the
example résumé (15) reveals, the letter résumé tends to contain
superfluous words and is therefore more difficult to read—even
though this example is an excellent selling letter.

Candidly, I hope you'll use the suggested outline since I think
it will get your story across faster and better. Regardless of the
outline you finally follow, use the graphic techniques found in

the résumé guide to make the key facts about you stand out. This will help you to establish yourself in the eyes of your prospective boss as an organized, clear-thinking businessman.

4 | How to Make
Your Interviews Pay Off
in an Offer

GIRDING YOURSELF FOR THE LION'S DEN

There's hardly a job-seeker I know who won't admit under questioning that he's blown at least one interview, maybe more. What do I mean by blown? Simple: he was unprepared for a tough question thrown at him, got sidetracked on a minor hangup of his prospective boss, came away knowing he wouldn't be invited back for a second interview, or knew he wouldn't be offered the job he thought he should get.

If you have blown a job interview, when you finish reading this chapter you'll probably know the reason why. If you haven't blown an interview, but think there's a chance you might, this chapter can probably help you to avoid making the simple errors that lead to disastrous interviews.

Not long ago I asked a job-seeker what he thought was the purpose of an interview. His response bears repeating: "An opportunity for a job candidate and his prospective employer to meet. To see if they like one another. To see if the candidate's background and the prospective boss's needs mesh."

There is probably no question that the key function of an interview is the determination by both job candidate and prospective boss of the fit of their respective needs and personalities. As I see it, however, interviews can be, and should be, much more. If you want to make interviews work harder for you than for the eighteen other candidates for the job, you ought to make them a live demonstration of your ability to:

1. Organize your thoughts.
2. Relate yourself to your prospective boss's problems.
3. Think on your feet.
4. Communicate your thoughts orally, and, most important,
5. Prove that you are a better man than your competition.

The ideas contained in this chapter should help you do all these things during your interviews. Do them naturally and instinctively so that even if your background and your prospective boss's job requirements do not totally mesh, you will still stand out as the best man he has interviewed, the man he feels will do most for his company, the man he feels the greatest body chemistry for.

At this point you are probably skeptical. "How can you make me stand out so well?" you might ask. In several ways. The first is by providing you with simple interview techniques that most job candidates don't think about, interview techniques that can make you a more effective interviewee. Here are a half-dozen of them.

1 / Look around your interviewer's office as soon as you get seated, before the interview begins.   Often a secretary will let you into your prospective boss's office prior to his arrival. Look around the room. Seek something interesting that you might talk about during the interview—a trophy that tells you your prospective boss shares a hobby with you (golf, bowling, tennis), a painting on the wall that suggests the geographic background of your prospective boss. A vice president of a leading company (one of the top ten in the United States) has in his office a number of marine decorations. A student of mine, taking an interview with him, asked about an antique ship's lantern on the wall. The question somehow led to the revelation that the vice president, a boating enthusiast, was originally from Newport, Rhode Island. The man taking the interview grew up in a small town close to Newport. The candidate was not, strictly speaking, a boating enthusiast. But he was knowledgeable about Newport, its regattas and home-town heroes. Much of the interview was spent on these topics. It shouldn't come as any surprise that the man from near Newport got the job.

2 / Be prepared to listen as well as talk. A common mistake of interviewees is that they think they are supposed to do most of the talking. While you can't get a job without opening your mouth, trying to monopolize the conversation can sometimes be a big mistake. In the first place, your prospective boss probably wants to hire a man who can listen as well as talk. In the second place, if you listen at the beginning of your interview, you may well pick up some ideas that will help you to relate your accomplishments to your boss's needs when it comes your turn to speak. Nothing is as sweet-sounding to a prospective boss as hearing how a candidate was able to solve problems similar to those that confront him. Even if you haven't solved any problems similar to those your prospective boss faces, you could still reveal your experience in trying to do so. Knowing that you are struggling with dilemmas akin to those your prospective boss is grappling with should endear you to him. (It's both of you against the world.)

Listen intently if your prospective boss wants to talk, even if it's for a long time. Take mental notes of each of his problems, if they are also your problems. Allude to them when you have an opportunity. (And you must make that opportunity, as explained in item 6.)

3 / Learn all you can about the companies you plan to interview. This thought seems so simple and so logical you'd think everyone would do it. But most people are too busy or too lazy to investigate the companies they interview, so the man who makes the effort is frequently a mile out in front of his nearest rival. Obviously you yourself haven't the time or inclination to investigate every company you write to or learn about from executive search firms. But if you manage to get an appointment for an interview, it's time to start digging for facts.

If you're going to interview a large company, in all probability you can get a copy of its annual report either at your local library or through a friendly stockbroker. It takes a couple of days to get an annual report from a broker, so leave yourself enough time. If the company you're going to interview is not a large one and hasn't issued an annual report, call the receptionist and ask whether or not someone in the firm has an annual report that can be sent to you—perhaps on a loan basis. Chances are your prospective boss will never know you called. Even if word gets back that you did, at least it shows your interest.

If you can't get hold of an annual report, you might have luck getting a recent market analyst's report. Usually these reports are on file at brokers' offices, so you should be able to get hold of one immediately as long as the company you interview is listed, or sold over the counter. If time is tight, your broker could even read it to you over the phone. The analyst's report is not as complete as an annual report, so use it only as a back-up source. A third source of information is Dun and Bradstreet. Many firms maintain contracts with D & B calling for issuance of as many credit investigations as the firm desires for a flat annual fee. If you're friendly with someone in the accounting department of your current firm, you may be able to get such a credit report at no cost to your current company, and at no cost to you. Usually these reports tell of sales and profit growth and give valuable profiles of key officers.

There is another alternative. If the company you're talking to is a major one, try looking through the pages of *Business Week, Nation's Business, Fortune,* or *The Wall Street Journal.* You may well run across a corporate ad which reveals the long-term objectives and strategy of the company. Your source of information makes no difference. The important thing is that you know something about the company you're going to visit. You should try to get a feel for what basic direction it intends to follow in the future, what its sales-growth rate has been, what its profit trend looks like, what successes and breakthroughs the company has made, and who its key executives are. And, most important, where its problems (or opportunities) lie.

4 / Get where you're going on time. This thought may seem excessively rudimentary. No doubt you follow it all the time. You'd be amazed, then, how many candidates show up late— twenty minutes, a half-hour, or even longer, without even so much as a phone call. If you are late, your prospective boss might well say to himself, "If he shows up late for his interview, he'll undoubtedly show up late for work too." So plan your route, if you haven't been there before. Phone your prospective boss's secretary to find out the best way to go. (A five-minute call could save an hour.) Don't get delayed or lost. Plan to be fifteen minutes early. You probably won't be. Even if you are actually early, you might do something for a few minutes so that you show up right at the appointed hour. Make your prospective boss think you are punctual and precise. Could be the other candidates were not.

5 / Dress as though you already had the job. It's a little embarrassing to bring up the matter of dress. Ninety-nine per cent of you have the common sense to dress correctly. For the one per cent who may have trouble deciding what to wear, a couple of points. Don't look as if you're going to a wedding. Don't look as if you're going to a baseball game. What then? Dress in the clothes you think your boss will wear. It's as simple as that. If your boss is likely to wear a sports jacket, you wear one too. If he's likely to wear a suit, a suit is for you. If your prospective boss interviews you in shirtsleeves, take your jacket off. One job candidate I coached told me that taking off his jacket was actually the key factor in getting his job. The man who interviewed him considered himself to be a real "shirtsleeves" worker. The job candidate felt uncomfortable in his jacket because his interviewer had on only a shirt and tie. The candidate asked if he could take off his jacket. That was it. The interviewer smiled and told him he was "his kind of man." From then on in it was duck soup.

During ten years of talking with job-seekers, I've suggested to several that they shave off their beards. This suggestion may make you think I'm an old fuddy-duddy. I'm really not. I don't give a damn if you have a beard or hair down to your shoulders. It's just that I hate to see a man put any obstacle in front of himself when it comes to getting a new job. If you suspect your prospective boss has a short haircut, you might as well get used to the fact that if you don't have one too, he might downgrade you—consciously or unconsciously. If you work for an advertising agency at which long hair may be in style, then your hair ought to be long. The point is this. Don't give yourself a black mark by wearing your hair long or sporting a beard if you suspect in the slightest it may be held against you. Get the job first. Then let your beard and your hair grow any which way. This suggestion may sound like an infringement on your personal freedom. Perhaps it is. But remember, you're looking for a better job. You don't want somebody else to get it. Give in a little with your ego—at least for the duration of your search.

6 | Plan in advance to control your part of the interview. Your primary objective in any interview is to let your prospective boss know that you are a man of accomplishment. A man of progressive accomplishment. A man with accomplishments that relate to his specific problems. With this thought in mind, somewhere in your interview you must find an opportunity to tell your prospective boss about your accomplishments. This may be easy. If your interviewer opens it up and says, "Tell me about yourself," go to it. If he asks you to give him a brief review of your background because he has mislaid your résumé, you have a perfect opportunity. Tell your prospective boss that, as you review your background, you'd like to let him know some of the more important contributions you have made along the way.

Sometimes it is a little more difficult to introduce your accomplishments. If your prospective boss asks you, "What makes you think you're the right man for us?" you might well want to answer, "I've got the right experience for the job." That's the wrong answer. Instead, say, "I've faced many of the same kinds of problems your company appears to face today. I believe my approach to those problems has been a successful one. Let me tell you about some of my contributions. You can judge for yourself."

And there you are. You tell him about the problem, what you did, and what happened as the result. He knows you are a guy who makes contributions. He figures you could make contributions for his company. Make a promise to yourself that you'll tell each person you interview the three accomplishments that appeal most to you and to those you have interviewed in the past. Don't leave without doing it.

HOW TO BE YOUR BEST SELF

A number of years ago I was asked to help an executive, then in his thirties, in his quest for a better job. In those days my help was limited strictly to résumé counseling. After a couple of sessions, this executive developed what we both felt was a fine résumé. Three months after our last session he called me. He was in trouble. His résumé was apparently working, because he was getting in the doors of the companies he wrote to. But he hadn't had a single nibble. Not one offer in all this time. I suggested he drop by to discuss his problem. Without warning him in advance, I used our session to simulate a job-interview situation. At the end of our simulated interview, I stunned him by saying, "Based on the last forty-five minutes, I wouldn't hire you on a bet." I went on to explain that he struck me as unnecessarily antagonistic. He challenged virtually everything I said. I admired his perceptive mind. I admired his questioning stance. But he made such a negative impression on me that I found myself continually on the defensive. And if that's the kind of impression this executive made on others, he would have a difficult time ever getting a job.

The key question of the day was what could be done for this executive to help him overcome his problem. In retrospect, the answer was simple enough. At the time I suggested it to him, however, neither of us knew if it would work. My suggestion was this: "For five minutes before you go into your next interview, program yourself to be your best self. Say to yourself, 'I'll give the interviewer the benefit of the doubt. I'll be more positive than I usually am. I'll question things just a little bit less than I normally do.' "

My suggested course of action was not designed to make over this executive. Not at all. It was intended to help him compensate for an obvious weakness, and in so doing reveal to his prospective boss his best self. I was sure that just thinking for five minutes about how negatively he came across would make him a little less abrasive during his interviews. Just being conscious of how he projected would make him just a tiny bit more sensitive to the effect of his questioning mind on the man who might become his boss.

Three days after our mock interview session, I received an ecstatic phone call from him. He told me that he had had two interviews with the same company in the two days after our meeting. During the second interview he was offered a job. He was unabashedly grateful. I was obviously heartened, although when you think about it, all I did was act as a sounding board to help him know how he came across to his interviewers. Now you might say that programing yourself to be a better interviewee is a hypocritical approach to take. You might well feel that if your prospective boss doesn't want you just the way you are, you really don't want to work for him anyhow. This alternative view is, I suppose, legitimate but I don't subscribe to it. When you read an ad for a new product or service, it sells the good things this new item or service brings. It doesn't dwell on the things that are not so good. You'll find out the not-so-good things when you investigate further. It's a sure bet, though, that you won't investigate at all if the good points of the product don't intrigue you first. For example, Volkswagen ads talk about fantastic mileage and economy, improved engineering year-to-year, high resale value. The ads don't tell you VW trunk space is ridiculously small. The ride is noisy, and wind resistance is nonexistent. You'll learn this when you take a test ride. Programing yourself prior to an interview has a single purpose. It shows your best self to your prospective boss. It gets him intrigued enough to check your references. He'll learn your bad points then. Don't worry. But he won't check your references at all if the only things he remembers about you are your weaknesses.

Had the suggestion I made to this executive not resulted in success for him, I never would have made it again. The fact that he managed to land a job only two days after our discussion, following so many unsuccessful interviews, however, led me to investigate interview techniques further. I asked friends who had interviewed job candidates what mistakes were most commonly made by them. Then I began to simulate interviews with all the people who came to me for help with their résumés. I was anxious to see whether they too were making mistakes that could be corrected. My investigation led to three conclusions. A lot of good men were missing getting good jobs simply because they didn't present themselves in the most favorable light during their interviews. Most of then were unaware of the problems inherent in their interviews. Most, if not all, of the problems were correctable once they surfaced.

To help you sell your best self, try the following two-step program: First, have someone help you identify your interview weaknesses. A friend you see infrequently or a friend of a friend is the best person to help you do this. If a friend can arrange for an interview with someone in your field who is willing to review his reaction to you, so much the better. This objective third party is likely to provide the best appraisal of your personal selling techniques.

If you don't have an objective friend, there's another alternative. Frequently in your job-seeking campaign you'll receive letters from companies or executive recruiters who state:

> We don't have a job opening suited to your experience at this time. However, we would like to meet you so that we may know more of your background in the event an opportunity for which you are suited does become available.

If you have the opportunity to meet someone who doesn't have a job opening for you, you have a perfect chance to review with him what he really thinks of you. After the formal interview is over, say to him, "Since we're not talking about a specific opening at this time, may I ask a small favor of you? Would you give me a critique of my interview style? It could help me in future interviews."

This is a flattering opportunity to be helpful. Most executives will be more than willing to do this much to help you in your job search.

After you have identified any interview weaknesses you may have, you're ready for step two. I call it your "Personal Compensation Plan." Five minutes before your next interview, think about what you can do to minimize that weakness. That's all. Just being conscious of the problem is enough to help you avoid it without changing the real you. Listed below are the more common negative impressions many interviewees make and how you can minimize them.

1 / You don't appear enthusiastic. Once when I was taking an interview I realized that I had done a strange thing. As we reviewed the plans that the company I was talking to had for marketing a new product, I said, "Well, the first thing we might do, is. . . ." The strange thing was that I was so wrapped up in my prospective boss's business problems, I suggested what we might do even though I was not a member of the firm. Afterward it struck me how enthusiastic I must have sounded. I resolved, from that point forth, to use the word "we" when referring to a prospective boss's problems which might become my own.

Given a choice between a man who is exceptionally bright but not particularly enthusiastic over the job I have to offer, and a man almost as bright but tremendously excited about my company and the job opportunity, I'd be inclined to take the second man. Why? Because I know he'd give the job his utmost, while I'm less sure about the first man. If you are inherently enthusiastic, you've got a lot going for you. However, if enthusiasm is not your middle name, then you ought to do something about it. Not to change yourself, mind you, but to make your lack of enthusiasm less obvious. And, as I said before, it's simple. For five minutes, promise yourself to look bright-eyed and bushy-tailed, to reflect enthusiasm, to comment positively on what your prospective boss may be talking about. To use the word "we" when you have a chance. To be encouraged about the potential opportunity. Even if you're not sold on every last element of your prospective boss's plans, try not to sound skeptical. When you get the job, you will have a chance to change the elements that concern you. But if you make a big deal about the things that you don't enthusiastically endorse, you may never get an opportunity on the job to make the changes you'd like to make.

2/ You overwhelm your prospective boss. Three years ago I interviewed a young man for a job in my department. He literally bounded into my office. He could barely restrain himself while I described the job to him. When he was given the chance to talk, he took off like a Boeing 747. His exploits were perilous. His solutions were a match for those of Jack Armstrong. He reminded me more of a high-school cheerleader, than a business-man. I wondered how well he would fit into our group. How well he'd listen at meetings. How much of a team man he would be. All in all, he struck me so much as a junior superstar that I was afraid to hire him in case he overwhelmed the people with whom he'd be working. If you tend to overwhelm, five minutes before your next interview promise yourself that you will be a little more diffident, sell yourself a little less aggressively, listen a little more, and promote your cause with just a little less bravado.

3 / You appear anxious, nervous.   Anybody who isn't nervous at a job interview probably hasn't any brains at all. After all, you don't know the person you are about to meet. You only know that in the balance lies your opportunity to get a better job. If you appear overly nervous, you can appreciate how your prospective employer may feel. He may look on a calmer candidate as fitting in better with his organization. If you appear nervous, smoke cigarette after cigarette, tap your fingers on the desk or chair, play with a key chain, or show any other nervous sign, tell yourself to hide it in the next interview. Rest your hands on the arms of the chair firmly. Resolve to do without a cigarette until after the interview. Tell yourself this, "You are ahead of the eighteen other men competing for this job because you know how to get a better job quicker." And before you finish this book you'll have ready answers to the ten toughest interview questions as well as knowing how to handle yourself in the most difficult interview situations. You can afford to be confident because you can and will get the job you want. In a word, five minutes before your next interview, tell yourself you know more about job-seeking than any of the eighteen other candidates you compete with. And give 'em hell.

4 / You appear over-relaxed, flip, or nonchalant.   If you have a couple of job offers in the bag, you may tend to be pretty relaxed about interviews. You may come across so relaxed that you blow the one opportunity you want most. Whatever the reason, if you project as being too relaxed (to the point that you seem not to care), tell yourself five minutes before your next interview that your other job offers fell through and you've lost your current job to boot. With that to shock you, chances are you'll appear genuinely interested. And your prospective employer is more likely to be interested in you.

5 / *You talk too much, too little, too loudly, or too softly.* Back in school I had to take a course in public speaking, in which each of us gave a recorded speech. Afterward we listened to ourselves. One thing was obvious to me during that playback session. I spoke too fast. Even today, if I am not thinking about it, I speak too fast. Most of us don't notice our speech patterns unless we use a tape recorder. But a friend or business associate might. So ask one how you come across when you speak. Once you know if you have a speech weakness, remind yourself of it before your next interview. It should largely correct itself. While you're considering your speaking habits, you might also want to consider your propensity to dominate the conversation. Some people talk too much, others not enough. Once you know which side you err on, plan to do the opposite. You'll probably end up talking just the right amount.

This list of weaknesses is not meant to be all-encompassing, just to bring to mind the most common personality faults that I've bumped into. You may learn that yours are unusual as you run through practice interviews with friends and business associates. The important thing to remember is that, once you know your weaknesses, they can be corrected to a large degree by simply thinking about them. If you have several weaknesses, you might want to jot down a key word or two for each. There is no doubt that you could put all your weaknesses on a very small scrap of paper. Look at it in the reception room. Whatever you do, don't go to any lengths to change yourself. Just look at your scrap of paper. If you note your weaknesses, they will change themselves for the better. And you'll be yourself—your best self.

5 | Good Answers for Good Questions

When you do well in an interview, you know it. You walk out of the office with your shoulders tall. You know your prospective boss was impressed. You know you'll be invited back. When an interview doesn't go well, you know that too. You don't like the answers you gave to the questions you were asked. You felt a strain develop between you and the interviewer. You say to yourself, "I wish I had it to do over again. I'd know what I should have said."

Some interviews are more difficult than others. In large measure, the degree of difficulty depends on the questions your prospective boss asks you. Some questions are genuinely tough. Tough enough to upset you and hence to lead to a sense of strain between yourself and your interviewer. In point of fact, these questions are frequently designed by the interviewer just to help him test your ability under fire. In my many discussions with executives following interviews, I have come across a number of questions that seem especially tough to answer. This chapter deals with ten of them. The answers given here to these ten questions aren't necessarily the only ones. But they work.

They've been tried. They can make what could be a difficult moment during an interview a whole lot easier on you. A word of caution in providing these answers. Put them in your own words. Understand the basic idea behind each. Don't memorize the answers. Let them be yours.

1 / Why do you want to leave your current affiliation? There are several good answers to this question. The first and most obvious is "I want to earn more money." No one ever knocked this answer. For most people, leaving their current affiliation will net them more than they could make in their next raise. Typically, the company that hires you away will pay 15 to 20 per cent more than you are now making to get your talents. In contrast, at your own company you can count on an annual raise of between 6 and 8 per cent. Of course, some executives use outside job offers as leverage to get more money from their present employers, but most of us will earn 6 to 8 per cent more each year where we work. The second, and equally good, answer to the question of why you want to leave is this: "Because I've ceased to learn. I'm looking for a job where I can grow as well as contribute."

This answer is in no way intended to knock your current employer. You're strongly advised never to knock your current employer. It simply means this: you're the kind of person who wants to learn while he works. At your current level of development you've mastered the job at your present company to the point where it's too easy for you. You're seeking a greater challenge than is available to you in your current job. A third answer to the "why do you want to leave" question is this: "My present company's growth hasn't been as fast as my own personal growth. This means that there are fewer chances for promotion within than are required to fulfill my personal ambitions."

This answer has two virtues: It suggests that you are personally ambitious. It suggests too that, were the company you are now with to grow faster, you would succeed and you would be promoted. It becomes a question of the timing being wrong. The simplest of these answers is "I want to earn more money." If you can use this answer, it's probably your best bet. The other two will get you by, however. Whatever you say, don't tell your prospective boss that you want to leave because your current company is no damned good. Why? If you feel your present company is no damned good, what will you feel like after a few years with the company you are now interviewing? Your prospective boss may well get the idea that you are not satisfied for very long, and his company will be next on your blacklist.

2 / What are your growth prospects at your current company? If you answer this question quickly, without giving it enough thought, you may come out with an answer that could hurt your chances of landing a job. If, for example, you answered, "Not too good. I'm boxed in; that's why I'm looking for a new job at this time," you'd be falling into a trap. Your interviewer must assume that you're not the best man at your company. Otherwise you'd know how to get out of the box. What you have to do is convince your prospective boss that you're leaving *in spite of* the fact that you are the best man at your current company. There are several things you might say to put the situation to your advantage.

> In the long run I think my chances are excellent. It largely depends on how soon my boss is promoted. His boss has been with the company twenty years and has another seven to go before he retires. So I'd have to wait quite a long time for my boss to move up. I don't know if I'm quite ready to wait it out. I know I have the opportunity to move up. It's a question of timing.

> The fact is I'm in line for a promotion. The real problem lies in our company's growth. When I joined, it was growing much faster than it is today. The way it now looks, all of us will have to wait some

time for the company to grow enough to justify any new senior positions. So my chances look good if we can get the company going again. But I don't know if I'm willing to wait. It's just a matter of timing.

In each of these examples, the job candidate places himself as a man ready to be promoted, or capable of being promoted, but unable to get a promotion when he wanted because of circumstances beyond his control. If your prospective boss thinks your chances are good at your current company, he'll be more inclined to think your chances are good at his company. And he'll be more inclined to hire you.

3 / What are your greatest strengths?   For some people this is an easy question. They know precisely their strengths and have examples at their fingertips to support each. But for many interviewees the question comes as a bit of a shock. And they seem flustered for a few moments while they collect their thoughts. It would be presumptuous of anyone to tell you your own greatest strengths. Only you can do that. But there are a few strengths that, if they are yours, are worth mentioning. Why? Because they are the most wanted strengths in the business world.

• Enough brains. Some people call it intellect. Others, intelligence. Some people say they're smart enough to handle the situation. Others prefer to say, "I have enough brains." Businesses need people with brains. And people with brains enough to know they have brains—and brains enough to let prospective bosses know this fact when they are asked.

• Drive. Or the ability to work long and hard, not only when the chips are down, but as a general rule. Some people become so involved with their professions that they think about them twenty-four hours a day. If you're the sort of person who can't leave the office at the office, let your prospective boss know. You are worth two men who quit thinking at five.

● Common sense. While there's no doubt you have to have brains in order to succeed in business, not every person with brains does succeed. Why? Because some people don't use their brains well. Common sense is the ability to nose out the core problem and to tackle it, to avoid the peripheral aspects of the business, to go right to the meat of the matter. If you have horse sense, your prospective boss should know about it.

● Maturity. Two things stand out as examples of maturity: First, the ability to establish work priorities, to know where to place your effort when all of a sudden many things must be done at once. Second, the ability to assess not only business problems but the relationship of people to these business problems. To recognize how those with whom you work react to their problems and to one another.

● An ability to deal with people. The smartest people are not necessarily the most successful people. The ability to relate to people, to encourage people, and to need people can sometimes overcome brains and common sense. If you have a natural talent in this area, your prospective boss ought to know it.

● Knowledgeability. Obviously, every prospective boss looks for men with industry experience similar to his own, or, at least, with functional job experience similar to that of the job he is seeking to fill. He knows it is easier to train a man who already knows his business. If you and your competition have almost equal knowledge, however, then your other strengths—brains, maturity, etc.—will be much more important than your knowledge.

In highlighting these most wanted strengths, again a caution: Flaunt them only if you have them. Do not mention them just because they're listed here. And be prepared to back up all your strengths with anecdotes that support your assessment of your strong points.

4 | What do you consider to be your greatest weaknesses? This is one of the toughest questions faced by job interviewers, and most particularly if you're unprepared for it. Yet it is a question that does come up, and you should have an answer which helps to sell you. Typically, unprepared job candidates answer this question in a way that hurts their chances. For example, a job-seeker might say, "I'm not good with figures." Or, "I sometimes have difficulty with people." Or, "Sometimes I tense up under pressure." Each of these answers, as well as others you can think of, makes you look less good in the eyes of your prospective boss. So the secret of answering this question, is to find negative traits your boss would like you to have. Here are some "positive weaknesses" which you can talk about if you have them. They cannot be faked.

● Impatience. Impatience with other people. Impatience with yourself. Impatience to get the job done. There's no question that impatience is a weakness. But it's a great one to have. You're impatient with other people because they don't get their part of the job done in time. Putting it another way, you want to see the whole job done when it's due. You're impatient with yourself because you're not growing fast enough. Putting it another way, you have a strong desire to grow in stature. You are ambitious. You want to grow in knowledgeability and in maturity. What boss could be disappointed with a man who is striving to improve himself? You're impatient to see the job done. Loosely translated, you have a sense of urgency about your job, a sense of concern about moving the corporation ahead. A fault your prospective boss by all rights should admire.

● Overdrive. This weakness is closely related to impatience. Perhaps one leads to the other. You drive yourself hard, perhaps overly hard. Your wife tells you you don't know when to stop. Sometimes you drive others the way you drive yourself. You push yourself to the extent of your own capacity, and sometimes even more. While overdrive is a fault, particularly when your own overdrive leads to pushing others, it is certainly an admirable fault. Why? Because it can only lead to moving the business ahead. What prospective boss wouldn't like a man working for him who does the work of two, because he drives himself so hard?

● Tendency to overview. Given a choice, you prefer to try to put all the pieces together, rather than to look at any particular piece. You prefer an assignment involving a broad analysis of a problem, rather than detailed administrative duties. This is a most acceptable weakness, since it makes you a prime candidate for a leadership position with your prospective company. Most top-echelon executives do seek out the big picture and leave minutiae to smaller minds. Even if overviewing is a fault of yours, don't say you can't handle details, because, even when you get to the top, you have to handle some details—just different ones. Rather, tell your boss you prefer to consider big concepts rather than minute specifics.

● You're hard to please. The status quo doesn't necessarily satisfy you. You sometimes question the world about you. You don't satisfy as easily as the next man. While no one likes a totally negative employee, you'll probably agree that the man who challenges what is going on about him is better than the man who accepts everything blindly and without question. Because the man who sees what's wrong has the opportunity to correct and amend it. The man who doesn't consider the alternatives can make no changes at all. Don't be afraid to say that you are hard to please. Most top executives are. Probably your prospective boss is.

● Stubbornness when you're right. There are no two ways about it. When you have the facts, you stick to your guns. You don't give in. This doesn't make you the most popular man on campus, but you don't mind running the risk of upsetting a few people. It's a lot easier to say "Yes." People like it better, and life is simpler. But you prefer to make your life a little more difficult when you are convinced you have the facts on your side. You will give in. But you don't like to let go until you're absolutely sure that the alternative is more correct than your own idea. Stubbornness is a genuinely undesirable trait, since others may resent it. But if you have to have a weakness, stubbornness isn't a bad one to have, since the opposite of stubbornness is a lack of conviction. The man who sticks to his guns has to have guts. He's never wishy-washy on the job.

Before leaving the question of your greatest weaknesses, there are several points that should be made. First, you don't necessarily have to discuss them all. If you get asked about your weaknesses, cite one or two. Second, if you don't fall heir to the weaknesses described above, by all means don't mention them. But if some of these faults are really you, don't be ashamed of them. There's good in each. Third, keep in mind a positive example of each weakness. For example, the man who is stubborn might have saved his company $100,000 because he refused to buy a piece of equipment when he thought alternative equipment would be superior. He may have fought with mid-management, and even top management because of his conviction. The proof of the pudding is the results of his stubbornness. His machine outperforms the other machine by a wide margin and saves a hundred grand. A strong positive accomplishment story related to your greatest weaknesses can turn a minus into a plus for you.

5 / *What do you want to be five years hence?* If you answer that you'd like to be president, you're terribly unrealistic—unless, of course, you happen to be an executive vice president now. Very few prospective bosses are looking for ninety-day wonders, men in mid-management who can assume the presidency in less than five years. And you look naïve if you answer

that way. You are being hired for your expertise at your present level. To presume that you will rise through the ranks like a rocket, passing others by, is presumptuous to say the least. On the other hand, few prospective bosses are looking for men who expect to sit still for five years, happily contented doing what they're doing now. In order to avoid extremes when you answer this question, you might say, "In five years I would like to be in my boss's job, with prospects of being in his boss's job in the not too distant future." There is a good reason for answering the question this way. You should expect to be in your boss's job within five years. If you can't make it in that time, you are hardly the man your boss should hire. At the same time, if you think you should be close to securing his boss's job in that period of time, you are exhibiting a realistic optimism and a reasonable amount of personal ambition.

6 / Do you mind taking a personality test prior to joining our company? The answer to this question should be obvious: "No, not at all."

Why should the answer to this question be so obvious? If it's asked at all, you can be darn sure that there's a policy which states that *every new employee* will take a battery of psychological tests. There's no point in saying "No" if you're at all interested in the job.

Some people rebel against personality tests. There, you might consider two things. First, the fact that they are given should not necessarily condemn the company you are interviewing. Frequently these are the tools used by Personnel as a matter of record to determine for future use what kind of employees stay with a company longest and do the best. They are generally not relevant to the decision to hire you or another man. Second, if you are concerned about taking such psychological exams, you might spend a few minutes reading the appendix to William H. Whyte Jr.'s *The Organization Man,* published by Simon and Schuster. It provides a brief (five-page), interesting commentary on personality testing. You'll feel better prepared and more confident when you take yours.

7 / *What do you want to make on your next job?*   (Or, "What are your salary requirements?") Your answer to this question depends on when it's asked. If it's too soon, perhaps on the first or second interview, you're better off begging the question. If this company has "the" job you're looking for, why state a salary requirement that might knock you out of the ball game simply because it makes you an unknown yet premium-priced player. If you are asked your salary requirements early in the game, why not say, "That depends on the job. I'd rather talk about finances after we've decided together whether I'm the right man for this job." Let them be convinced you are the only man they want. Your bargaining position will be that much stronger. Don't let your prospective boss use your salary requirement as a factor in determining whether he wants you. Let him use your salary requirement as a personal challenge after he's decided he must have you.

If you're asked your salary requirement on your third or fourth interview, or after your prospective boss has expressed very keen and specific interest in you, give him the answer he seeks. Forthrightly. Positively. *Not* apologetically. Not as a question. You should expect a 20 per cent increase when you leave your current concern to join another company in a similar capacity. This figure, of course, depends on the economic situation. But remember this: A company expects to pay a premium for going on the outside. They expect to pay for training by some other firm. When you're on the job, you will probably not receive more than a 6, 7, or 8 per cent annual increase. So ask for at least 20 per cent more than you're currently making. If you feel confident of their interest in you ask for 25 per cent. The important thing is this: When your prospective boss has been sold on you as his first choice, he'll pay a little bit more to make sure he gets you. Your first job is to make sure he wants you.

8 / What are you currently making?   To most people this is not a difficult question. They are pleased to state their current salary, recognizing that it will be considered in their prospective boss's own salary offer. (These people figure correctly that they will be offered at least as much by the prospective boss, and frequently more.) For two groups of people, however, the question concerning current salary is a tough one.

The first group of people is those who are currently underpaid. Chances are they are considering leaving their current jobs simply because they are underpaid. These people are concerned that if they reveal their lower-than-fair current salary it will lead to a low-ball offer from their prospective boss. These people are also concerned that their current low salary suggests they have less responsibility than they really do.

The second group of people who are concerned about the "What is your current salary?" question are those executives who have a financial package of which salary is only one part. Those people may be paid a bonus and have stock options on top of their salary. Obviously, if a company you are interviewing offers only salary, you have to take this into consideration, since you will lose out on the cash value you received from a bonus and/or stocks.

• For those who are currently underpaid: Tell your prospective boss your current salary without hesitation. And then add, audibly, "That's precisely the reason I am here today." Let your prospective boss know you know you are underpaid by industry standards; that you're leaving your current employer because you want to make a wage comparable to that of others in similar jobs in your industry. Your prospective boss should get the idea quickly.

• For those of you who are currently receiving a comprehensive financial package: Tell your prospective boss what your current salary is and then add, "The total value of my current financial package is . . . This is made up of the following: my stock is worth . . . my guaranteed bonus is . . . my incentive bonus is worth . . ." It is not a reality to consider your current earnings based on salary alone, since no matter how or when you are paid, it's the total value that counts, not the bits and pieces.

9 / What do you think of your current boss? Sometimes an interviewer will ask you point blank what you think of your current boss, or perhaps the president of your company. When this occurs, you can pretty much count on your prospective boss knowing your current boss, or the president, personally through a trade organization, or by reputation. In this case, your prospective boss is undoubtedly trying to find out, among other things, whether your opinion of the man in question is similar to his own. I personally think it's an unfair question. But it is asked, nonetheless. If you are confronted by this question, be positive even if it hurts. If you think the president is a tyrant, say instead, "Our president is an extremely strong leader. He's firm in his handling of people and a demanding executive." Whatever you do, don't give an emotional response, even if you think the president is a son-of-a-bitch. The reason is simple. Your prospective boss is not only trying to find out if your judgment agrees with his, but also whether or not you're a loyal employee. Be honest in your appraisal of the man in question, and couch your thoughts in words that should come from a loyal employee.

10 / What actions would you take if you came on board? Your initial response might be to describe the changes you would make if you were hired to fill the position you're interviewing for. Suppress that inclination, and don't do it. Instead, say that the chances are likely that you wouldn't do very much at all for a while. Not at least until you had a chance to really evaluate the situation from the inside. After all, it's most difficult to determine a course of action without having been totally immersed in the problems. The old adage "Fools rush in where angels fear to tread" certainly fits here. If you wish, there is nothing stopping you from adding, "If the situation turns out to be what I think it might be, I might take the following type of action. . . ." Whatever you do, don't look like a whirling dervish who has come in to change an organization before he's had a chance to see what's good about it.

There will undoubtedly be other difficult questions that you will face on job interviews. Perhaps questions related to your own particular background. While we obviously can't discuss the answers without knowing the questions, two last thoughts:

• Whatever the question, try to answer it in the most positive manner, particularly if it is in regard to your current affiliation. Whatever the question, try to turn weaknesses into strengths. Whatever the question, be as honest in your answer as you possibly can. If nothing else, you'll be admired for that.

• If you come across a tough question, one that throws you, make a note of it right after the interview. Think about it for as long as it takes for you to come up with a reasonable answer. And tuck it in the back of your mind. It probably won't come up again, but if it should, it makes life a whole lot easier to have a well thought out answer—and one in which you have confidence—rather than to have to think out your answer on the spot, under pressure, all over again.

A SUGGESTION: Reread this chapter in a couple of days. Fix in your mind the questions and the answers suggested here which are appropriate to you. Consider this chapter much as you would a practice college entrance exam in your junior year. It's intended to help prepare you today for what interviews may be like tomorrow. It should give you confidence that you won't be coming up against tough questions cold turkey. Even if you can't subscribe to all of the answers given here, at least you'll start thinking of your own responses before the question is asked.

STOP

6 | Tough Interview Situations — How to Take Them in Stride

It happened ten years ago. But it's so vivid in my mind you'd think it took place yesterday. It was undoubtedly the worst interview I ever had. My interviewer was an executive recruiter. As soon as I entered his office, I had a feeling I would blow it. After glancing over my résumé, the recruiter spent a half-hour trying to convince me I should not leave my current company. Since I thought the choice of whether to switch jobs was mine, I literally battled with him. His insistence annoyed me. I countered his arguments with every logical reason I could think of. Within ten minutes there was an acrid atmosphere in the room. We never did discuss the job opening he called me about. I went away feeling he was either damned stupid or a bastard.

Throughout the day I thought over what had happened that morning. By the end of the day I had convinced myself that the executive recruiter was retained by my current company and, among other things, was obligated to persuade all people considering leaving not to do so. The following morning I phoned him and confronted him with my theory. He assured me that he was not retained by my current company and, in fact, he knew no one there and had taken his perverse tack at our interview to see what I was like when I was angry. He said that as an interview technique he always adopted a belligerent stance and frequently argued with job-seekers about why they wanted to leave their current firms. Then I realized what had taken place. *I had allowed myself to get suckered into an interviewer's trap.*

In subsequent years I thought a lot about this disastrous interview. I concluded that, had I realized what the interviewer was trying to do, I not only could have avoided the confrontation, but actually could have turned that interview into a positive personal sale. The objective of this chapter is to help you avoid some of the typical mistakes interviewees make simply because they don't assess the interview situation correctly, and thus are unable to respond to it in a way that promotes their cause.

Here are ten tough interview situations that might well face you in your job search, and some suggestions on handling them.

1 /

PROBLEM.   The man who is interviewing you doesn't open his mouth. The man you thought would keep the interview going leaves it all up to you. The silence is depressing. You answer the questions your prospective boss asks, but there's a long pause between the answer to your last question and his next question. You come away disappointed with your performance. You didn't seem to be able to establish a rapport.

ANALYSIS/ACTION.   It shouldn't take more than one long pause for you to know your interview is not pacing itself as it should. The silence is deafening. After two seemingly endless pauses, prepare yourself to carry the conversation, to take your interviewer off the hook. Suggest to your prospective boss that you'd like to review for him the accomplishments in your current job that you think qualify you for this one. And then keep talking. Talk specifically. Talk anecdotally. Talk about your accomplishments. But keep talking. Why? Your interviewer may be inexperienced, may not know how to keep the conversation going. If this is the case, he will be truly grateful to you for making the interview a success. It's possible also that your prospective boss is just plain taciturn and emotionally unable to conduct a warm and chatty interview. If this is the case, he'll also be grateful if you carry the ball. Not only your accomplishments will be remembered, but your ability to convey a sense of movement and warmth to a chilly and unmoving interview situation.

2 /

PROBLEM. *Your prospective boss won't stop talking.* He talks about his company. He talks about himself. He talks about the problems his company now faces. He talks about the prospects for the future. One thing seems for sure: he doesn't give you a chance to open your mouth.

ANALYSIS/ACTION. This kind of interview presents both an opportunity and a challenge. An opportunity, since it provides you with insight concerning the company you might be working with and the man you might be working for. This is the real bonus of such an interview. A challenge, because you know, if the job is worth while, you have to make your prospective boss believe you are the exceptional man among the many he has interviewed. This interview is the only time you have in which to do it. The question is how, when your prospective boss doesn't seem to stop talking. One way is to ask for an opportunity to spend a few minutes talking about yourself. The key is to know when and how to ask. In my judgment, the best time is after you have given your prospective boss a chance to talk himself out, after you have given yourself a chance to make mental notes on two or three or four problems or future opportunities that your prospective boss wants to get off his chest. Then wait for a pause and seize your opportunity. Ask for a few minutes to talk about your accomplishments. Here's how you might do it: "Three of the problems you described interested me most. May I take a few minutes to tell you about several of my contributions at my current company in areas that seem to be of real interest to you?" You've done it. You've asked for a few minutes. You've asked to relate accomplishments or contributions. And you've promised to relate them to what interests your prospective boss. You just might be able to get him to stay quiet and give you a chance to talk. No promises, mind you. But if you didn't have the guts to ask, you'd be no better off. So it's worth the try!

A WORD OF CAUTION: It sometimes takes a lot longer than you think for your prospective boss to talk himself out. Don't interrupt, even if you think he's much more long-winded than you thought he would be. He'll have to unwind sometime and you'll get your chance to ask. If you doubt it, witness what happened only last year. An associate of mine learned of a job in Chicago. He flew there for a Saturday-morning meeting with the vice president of manufacturing. He met, as scheduled, with the vice president at 8:00 in the morning. The manufacturing VP proceeded to talk without pause for the next two and one-half hours, concerning his company, its problems and opportunities. At no point during this 150-minute marathon did the vice president once ask my associate if he would like to comment on his own experience in relationship to the problems faced by his company. At about 10:30, the VP invited my associate to tour the plant. This excursion lasted another hour. My associate sensed that the time was right. He asked if he might have an opportunity to talk a little bit about his experience and contributions in relation to the wealth of information the vice president had given him about his company. Naturally, the opportunity was granted. And my associate talked about his own experiences—to an avid listener—for an hour and a half. He had gone to Chicago thinking that his interview might last two hours. In actuality it had lasted five. As you might expect, he now works for this company.

3/

PROBLEM. The man who interviews you seems to have a personal dislike of you. Nothing you say pleases him. Examples: He asks you why you want to leave your current firm. When you tell him, he lets you know that's not much of a reason. He asks your experience with a particular kind of machine. When you tell him, he lets you know that several other candidates have more experience than you. You get no positive vibrations with this man. You feel miserable. You are certain you failed with him.

ANALYSIS/ACTION. No matter how much your interviewer taunts you, keep your cool. Chances are he wants you to lose it. He wants to see how you are in a stress situation. This kind of interview is not common today. Nonetheless, some interviewers still enjoy seeing men squirm. It's up to you. You can be the man who doesn't squirm, if you try. How do you go about this? Simple: every time he knocks your contributions or responds negatively to your answers, agree with him. At the same time, suggest that you have made other contributions you would like to tell him about. For example: if he tells you your experience on a particular machine isn't as good as that of other candidates he's interviewed, say, "You're probably right. But the $64,000 question is will I make contributions for your company. Now when I was working on the machine [in question], we faced a real rough problem. What I suggested was. . . . And the problem was solved." In a nutshell, your strategy is to keep him on your track, the anecdotal accomplishment track. Don't let him drag you onto his. No matter how hard he puts the screws to you, don't argue with him. Agree with him. Perhaps he's right. Then direct him back to your accomplishments. It may not be easy. But two things are for sure. First, you won't get anywhere arguing with your prospective boss. No candidate ever won an argument before he was hired. Who needs that kind of guy on the payroll? Second, if you can hold out in spite of the structured stress, your prospective boss will at least think of you as the one man who remained calm and level-headed while pressures were exerted on him. And that's not a bad way to be remembered.

There's one instance where you can feel free about arguing with your prospective boss. That's when it's a matter of principle.

If he raises an important issue—such as politics, religion, ethics, etc.—in which you have a strong and opposite point of view, you should tell him that you don't agree. There's no sense in letting him think you would work for him if you could not see eye-to-eye on a matter of basic principles.

At this point I'm frequently asked; "Why not argue with this interviewer? You wouldn't want to work for him anyhow. What difference does it make if you give it back to him as hard as he gives it to you?"

The answer is this. One interviewer does not a company make. It may well be that this style of interview is the particular favorite of someone you must meet during the interviewing process, someone with whom you'd work very infrequently. Unless structured stress is the operational device of the man whom you would work for directly, it would be unfair to assume that you wouldn't enjoy working for this company. However, you might well want to check with friends or associates who could give you a better insight into the working life at this company.

4 /

PROBLEM. The interviewer starts the interview by quickly looking over your résumé. Then he proceeds to ask you an endless list of questions, many of which are difficult and some of which can be found in the previous chapter on tough questions. You can almost feel your adrenal glands at work. Your palms begin to get sweaty. You weren't quite prepared for the rapidity with which these questions are asked, nor for the difficulty of providing single, clear answers to them.

ANALYSIS / ACTION. While the rapid-fire questioning technique is tough on you, it undoubtedly provides a benefit to your interviewer. It lets him know which of the candidates he sees are able to think on their feet and to think calmly under pressure. Your knowledge of some of the more difficult questions asked by interviewers will make it easier for you to think on your feet than it is for the man who hasn't been exposed to these questions before. It's sort of like taking the sample driving test prior to the real thing. There will, of course, be questions thrown at you that you don't have the answers for. When this happens, keep the following thoughts in mind:

● Answer questions by referring to specific accomplishments, if you can, in any way, shape, or form.

● If you don't know the answer to a particular question, say you don't know. You will at least be thought of as honest. That may be better than the next man.

● Don't get flustered. If the rapid-fire questions start to unnerve you, remember they'll unnerve the other candidates as well.

If you keep your cool when others can't, you'll be the stand-out candidate by default. It is a well-known fact that at the Harvard Business School ninety-five out of a hundred first-year students used to fail the first mid-course examination. They failed because the test was designed so that 95 per cent couldn't pass, no matter how hard they studied. Why did the faculty use such an unfair test? Probably to see how well students functioned after this kind of trauma. Your prospective boss may be trying to do something similar. No matter how frustrated you feel, don't panic. Remain honest and calm. Keep in mind the most important thing you have to sell: your contributions to sales and profits. No one can take them away from you. Remember that the interviewer who tries to pick a fight probably is looking for someone who knows how to avoid one.

5 /

PROBLEM. This interview deals exclusively with one subject: the company. Your prospective boss starts by asking you what you know about his company. Then he tells you a great deal about his company. He closes the interview by asking if you have any questions about his company. He skims over your experience. His primary focus is on his company and how you relate to it.

ANALYSIS/ACTION.   The one thing your prospective boss may care most about when he selects someone to work for him is the candidate's interest in or enthusiasm for the company he's hoping to join. As I said earlier it isn't a terribly difficult task to learn about a company you might work for for the rest of your life. Your prospective boss may just be looking to see if you've taken the necessary effort.

But in this instance your prospective boss is probably seeking more than a playback of what you know about his company from last year's stockholders' report. The single best chance you have to separate yourself from competition is when your prospective boss asks if you have any questions about his company. If you want to be the one who gets the job, you should have several cogent, well-thought-out questions on the tip of your tongue. Questions that show your interest in his company.

This task sounds tough, and is. But it really is easier for you than for your competition because you will recognize the interview situation as it progresses and can be prepared to ask your questions. How do you know the question on questions is coming? When you are confronted with, "What do you know about our company?" followed by a lecture on the very same topic, you can be damned sure it's about to happen. So . . . prepare yourself by making mental notes of those aspects of your prospective boss's business that relate to the specific contributions you have made in your current company.

When the time comes for you to ask your thoughtful questions use your own experience as a frame of reference. For example:

> You mentioned that one of the major problems confronting you at this time is the development of a new inventory control system. As my résumé suggests, I worked on a new control system for my current company which resulted in an inventory investment reduction of close to 20 per cent. Among the alternatives we considered was warehouse consolidation. Is consolidation a possible alternative your company has considered? What, if any, kinds of problems would consolidation result in for your business?

Questions as specific as these can do a lot to make you stand out favorably. First, they demonstrate genuine interest in your prospective boss's problems. Second, they relate your contributions to those specific areas in which your boss needs help.

6 /

PROBLEM.   Your prospective boss likes you. He tells you so. He's impressed with your contributions. He's impressed with you. But, and it's a very big but, your experience isn't specifically what he's looking for. In all probability he has met other candidates with experience slightly more in tune with his immediate needs than your own.

ANALYSIS / ACTION.   When you face a situation like this, you should consider taking two steps: First, agree with your prospective boss that your experience isn't as directly applicable as that of some other people who are probably applying for the job. Unless you have forgotten to include some relevant experience on your résumé that you are now ready to reveal, there is no point in trying to convince your prospective boss that your experience is precisely what he wants. He has already decided for himself that it is not. So why antagonize him during the balance of your interview?

Instead, lay out the alternatives for him in a way that perhaps he has not considered. This is not easily done. But you've nothing to lose by trying, so why not attempt it as your second step?

As I see it, Mr. Jones, you are confronted by three alternatives: First, you could take on a man like myself whose accomplishments seem to impress you but who hasn't had a particular experience you'd like him to have. Second, you could select a man with fewer accomplishments to his record but with 'just the right' experience. Third, you could wait a couple of months or perhaps even a year and see if you can't locate a man with the exact experience and the record of accomplishments you want. If I've summed it up fairly, Mr. Jones, could I comment about the situation?

If your prospective boss accepts your definition of the problem, you have a fighting chance of talking him into hiring you. You have convinced him that there are drawbacks to each alternative. In your case, not quite the experience he seeks. In the case of the man with the exact experience, not quite your list of accomplishments. In the case of the man with both experience and accomplishments, an indefinite delay until he's found. After defining the problem, the time has come to try to persuade your prospective boss that your alternative is the best one. Your strategy is to talk the future—specifically, what the situation might be in a year's time:

> Mr. Jones, while I have a little less experience than my competition, in a year's time I think you'll be happier having hired me than the men I'm competing against. As my record indicates, you know whatever I've tackled I've done well. In a year's time I believe I will have caught up on the experience, and perhaps even contributed more to your business than my competition, who now has more experience but not more contributions. If you elect to wait for "the" man with a record of contributions as well as the exact experience you seek, you might end up waiting a year to find him. So perhaps hiring me now would be a pretty good alternative. I won't lack for trying!

Obviously this approach won't work every time. But if you are up against a strong bias of "not quite the right experience," you at least have a logical way to attack it. You have found the Achilles heel in the argument that an experienced man would necessarily be better. It's worth a try.

The following interview situations differ from those above. This next group deals with three delaying situations: when you're trying not to get a job, or to delay a job offer or your acceptance. While these situations are not as critical as the former, nonetheless, knowing a reasonable solution to each before you find yourself in the situation may make you sweat a little less.

7 /

PROBLEM.   You've been called to an interview. Things have
gone amazingly well. You have an opportunity to relate your accomplishments. Your prospective boss is genuinely impressed.
You know his company well. And when you read over the annual report, you were excited about its prospects. You were enthusiastic when you came for your interview. Then it happened.
Your prospective boss described the specific job he has open.
You know it is not for you. You know it is not suited to your
professional experience or your career objectives or your salary
requirements. And this despite the fact that your résumé clearly
stated your job objective. You don't know whether the personnel
director chose to ignore it, or if the executive recruiter who told
you of this opening failed to send your résumé along. It doesn't
much matter. The point is, while you like the company very
much, the job now open is absolutely, positively not for you.
Your problem is to close the interview but keep a strong relationship with this company for the future.

ANALYSIS / ACTION.   If you're confronted with a situation like
this one, there are three things you ought to consider doing:
First, no matter how mad you feel inside, don't show it! It will
spoil your opportunity to take steps two and three, which are
worth hanging on for. Second, make sure your interviewer un-
derstands you are not at all interested in the job he's considering you for. Let him know you are sorry for any misunderstanding, but that, as your résumé states, you are seeking a different
kind of job from the one which he just described. The third step
is to try to convince your interviewer that, although he didn't
plan to fill the position you want, you are such a good man he
ought to reconsider his company's personnel needs and make a
position for you suited to your objectives. *This won't be easy.*
But it's worth a try as long as you've taken the time and the effort to get the interview. Here's how you might approach it:

Mr. Jones, thanks for describing the current opportunity you have
open. You know I'm very enthusiastic about your company and the

prospects you have outlined to me. But, in all candor, I must tell you there's been a misunderstanding between us. The position you're seeking to fill, while interesting, is not what I had in mind. It's really what I was looking for three or four years ago. I hope that you won't hold this against me, since I seem to have had a different understanding as to what the job was all about.

While it looks like you don't have an opening suited to my objectives at this time, maybe in the future your organization may need someone with my background. Let me review with you some of my experience and contributions so you can get an idea of my level of expertise and perhaps see where I might best fit in your organization.

Then sell your accomplishments, particularly at the organizational level you are trying to get the interviewer to hire you at. You may be surprised at the results. A month from now, if you're still looking for a job, you might well receive a call, as a friend of mine once did three weeks after such an interview, inviting you to talk about a new position at your level which "has just opened up."

It may well be that the new position is a genuine one. On the other hand, I know of many instances where positions were created around the man the company wanted. The companies were so anxious to obtain the talents of these executives that they reshuffled their existing organizations to make room for the individuals. While you can't count on such good fortune, don't disregard the possibility. Be prepared for an interview situation in which the job is not for you. Don't pack up. Go ahead and sell your accomplishments anyhow. Then lay it on the line as to the kind of position you want. You have nothing to lose and a potential job to gain.

8 /

PROBLEM.   You are on your third interview. Things are going well. You sense that the company is interested in you and that a job offer may well be forthcoming. You like the company. You might well work for it. But—and again, it's a big but—this company is your second choice. You are also interviewing another company, and you would prefer to work for it. Unfortunately, negotiations with the second company aren't as far along as those with the first. The first company calls you to a fourth interview and offers you the job. You are in a quandary. Should you accept the job at hand or hold out for the job you'd really like to have? What should you do?

ANALYSIS/ACTION.   What you really want from company #1 is some time to let you find out whether or not you will get a job offer from company #2. How do you get the time you need? By asking for it in an honest way. Point out that, when you relocate, you hope to stay a good many years, and you want to be sure you make the right decision. Let company #1 know of your negotiations with company #2 (without revealing its name), and the state of these negotiations. Let company #1 know that you could not accept a job with it in good conscience unless you have a chance to complete negotiations now in progress with both companies. It wouldn't be fair to you, nor would it be fair to company #1 if you hadn't thought out the problem in its entirety. You can ask for up to two weeks to make a final decision. That may seem like a long delay to the first company. When you consider, however, that it has been searching for some time, and it has committed itself to you, I think you'll be granted ten working days in which to arrive at a decision. Or at least a week. The important thing is this: If you let company #1 in on your problem, it is likely to keep open its job offer for a reasonable period of time while you wind things up with company #2.

You should then approach company #2 with the same honesty with which you approached company #1. Try and arrange a special interview. Explain the pressure being put on you. Ask company #2 if it can move up its decision date or let you know whether you are a prime candidate. If your prospective boss can't see you, give him a call, or write, telling him your problem. Ask for his counsel and aid.

If you are a highly-thought-of candidate at company #2, there's a very good likelihood it will move faster. If its interest in you is only moderate, it probably won't. In which case you have your answer. The chances of your being offered a job at company #2 are slim. You're better off to accept the original offer at company #1. After all, while it is your second choice, it wants you. That's worth a lot in the long run.

9 /

PROBLEM.   You arrive at your interview in good spirits. Your prospective boss is enthusiastic about his company. The information he provides you, plus your own research, suggests it is a company you'd like to work for. Your prospective boss tells you that he has no opening similar to the one you seek. He does have an opening at a lower level, however. He asks you to take the lower-level job, and after a certain unspecified period of time he will try to make a job opening suited to your background. In short, he promises you a fabulous future and asks you take a flyer at a job you really don't want until such time as he can make an opening suited to your needs and objectives. You like the company. You are perplexed over the proposition.

ANALYSIS/ACTION.   You may well be leary of opportunities such as this one, for several reasons. In the first place, you must somehow question an employer who is incapable of seeing how tough taking a step back is for you. Obviously you don't want a job at a lower level than the one you now have. If he is unable to see this problem, you may well ask if he would understand other problems, once you went to work there.

A second reason you may be leary of such a job is the nebulous way future plans are presented. Without assurances as to when and how you will be promoted, it's a risky proposition at best. Supposing you don't like the company after you join it? Certainly you don't want to leave in a position that's lower on the organization chart than the one you now have.

In view of the uncertainties of accepting a position you don't want for an indefinite period of time, you might try to persuade your prospective boss to offer you a job at least equivalent to the one you now have. Your chances of convincing him are obviously remote. But not impossible. Your best leverage is another job offer. If you have one, you might say to your prospective boss:

> Thank you for your offer, Mr. Jones. As you know, the future of your company intrigues me. I will mull it over very seriously, although right now my answer would have to be no, since I have a job offer suited to my experience level with the ABC Corporation, which is also a fine company. In all sincerity, were I to come to work for your company, I would be putting my career back a year or perhaps more. It's a less exciting opportunity for me since I have the ABC offer.
>
> While I'm mulling over your proposition, is there any possibility you might be able to dream up some change in your organizational structure that would make your proposition more enticing?

If you don't have a job offer, the chances of convincing your prospective boss are even more remote. If you are close to securing another job, you may be able to phrase your comments in such a way that your prospective boss gets the idea that you have a better offer.

If you can't persuade him to give you assurances of the specific time in which you will be promoted, or, better still, a position equal to that you now have, then my advice would be to keep looking.

10 /

PROBLEM. This interview is a novel one. *You don't do any talking.* Your prospective boss does it all. He tells you what a great company he works for. He tells you about its tremendous prospects. He waxes eloquently about the wonderful working conditions and the people. At the end of the interview, your prospective boss asks you when you could begin to work. You pinch yourself. Is this a dream? You didn't open your mouth and you got yourself a job offer, a seemingly great job offer!

ANALYSIS / ACTION. Perhaps I'm a born skeptic, but I'd be afraid of such an offer. If you are proferred a job without being asked to discuss your experience and accomplishments, you might smell a rat. It could be the job. The company may have serious financial or organizational problems ahead of it. If you find yourself in a situation in which you are asked to join the company on your first interview with no effort on your part, relax. Ask for time to think it over and investigate it thoroughly. Don't get caught in a job that turns out to be a bust.

7 | Writing Your Way to a Better Job

Not long ago someone I counseled on résumé and interview techniques asked me, "Just how important is it to learn to write good job-seeking letters?" The person then went on to say, "I really feel my résumé is damned good, and I'm sure I know how to make my interviews pay off. So just how valuable is a job-seeking letter anyhow?" Here's my answer.

A good job-seeking letter is definitely not frosting on the cake. It is a separate and distinct tool you need in order to get a better job quicker. A good job-seeking letter can get you in the interviewer's door in some cases where a résumé wouldn't get you over the threshold. A good job-seeking letter might well make a good interview be remembered as a superb interview by the man who talked to you. Most important, 90 per cent of the job-seeking letters I've seen over the years aren't worth the postage to mail them. If *you* can write a *good* job-seeking letter, you will be remembered as having written an outstanding one, since the others are so bad. This is not the case with your résumé, since your prospective boss is likely to see a number of good résumés along with your own.

This chapter reviews the four basic job-seeking letters you ought to write, and provides examples of each. Before looking at these letters individually, there are a few points relative to all good job-seeking letters:

• Good job-seeking letters relate to the reader's problems. In some cases you'll know the exact problems. In other cases, you can only suspect they exist. If you know the problem, so much the better. If you can only guess what it is, still include reference to it. Why? Because the reader is more interested in his problems than he is in yours. You can get his attention, and get it faster, if you talk about things that are near and dear to him —the problems he needs solutions for.

• Good job-seeking letters include at least one, and where possible several, of the writer's important accomplishments. Because you've already developed a list of your own contributions, written clearly and succinctly, you'll find that writing good job-seeking letters really is easy for you.

• Good job-seeking letters must appear as professional as the résumés that often accompany them. You would be appalled to see the number of scribbled letters, scratch-pad memos, and hunt-and-peck (x'd out) typed notes sent out by otherwise professional businessmen.

When you write letters as part of your campaign to get a better job quicker, you want those letters to sell the best you. How do you do this? Order businesslike stationery, good-quality, rag-content paper. Have your name and address printed at the top, as though you were a professional in business for yourself. In point of fact, on your job-seeking campaign, you are just that. Find someone to type the letters professionally for you—a friend, your wife, a public stenographer. Even if you pay a little for it, do it. You want to be thought of as a pro, not an amateur.

One final point about your professional-looking letters: Include your phone number. Have it printed below your name and address. Or include it below the initials of the typist at the bottom of the page. It matters not how you include your number as long as you do include it. You'd be surprised at the speed with which prospective bosses sometimes want to move. If they can't reach you, they might reach somebody else. By the time a letter arrives, somebody else may have been offered your job. Don't risk it.

• Good job-seeking letters avoid the common errors that turn off the readers you want to turn on. The most obvious of these is misspelling your prospective boss's name. You wouldn't believe how many job candidates fail to check the exact spelling of the name of the person to whom they're writing. No one has to tell you how important a man's own name is. And it only takes a minute or two longer to make sure the spelling on your letter is correct. Names aren't the only thing frequently misspelled in job-seeking letters. The other day I received a letter from a man who told me that he had just the right "experiance" for the position described in our ad. It may well be that this man had the right experience but he also didn't know how to spell. That's one weakness he need not have revealed so soon. Better leave it hidden until after you have the job.

A second, less frequent error is inclusion of a photograph. An important objective of job-seeking letters is to create curiosity and interest in you. When you send a photograph there's one less reason for meeting you. About the only people I know today who still include pictures on their memo pads are insurance agents. I am sure they have their reasons. But unless you're selling insurance, forget it.

JOB-SEEKING LETTERS YOU SHOULD WRITE

As part of your job-seeking campaign, you'll need to develop four letters that are essential to a professional search.

1 / Interview follow-up letters. The least-used and potentially most effective job-seeking letter is the one you send out following your interviews. Why most job-seekers fail to send a letter following every interview is a mystery to me. Perhaps the pressures of time are such that job-seekers give it a low priority. When you think about it, however, the interview follow-up letter can do a great many things for you.

• It will help you to be remembered. Chances are you'll be one of the few persons interviewed thoughtful enough to send a follow-up note. Your prospective boss will remember you when others are forgotten.

• It's an opportunity to reiterate that you understand your prospective boss's problems.

• It gives you a second chance to relate your past contributions to your prospective boss's current problems.

• It gives you an opportunity to show your genuine interest in the job opportunity. Read the letter below from candidate to prospective boss. It arrived in the mail two days after their interview. Consider what the prospective boss must have thought about this candidate.

```
Mr. A. J. Jones
President
The ABC Company

Dear Mr. Jones:

Thank you for the opportunity of meeting you yesterday to
discuss a career with the ABC Company.  In talking of the
many aspects of your company's phenomenal growth, I was most
impressed with your corporate philosophy concerning
acquisitions.

In this regard, thank you for the chance to review the role
I played in my own company's purchase of the XYZ Company
(now a subsidiary of our firm).  As we discussed, the XYZ
Company added more than 25% to our sales volume.  Naturally
I am proud of my part in consummating the purchase agreement,
particularly since the XYZ Company had been close to being
purchased by our chief competitor, and had decided against
the deal during negotiation.

Again, may thanks for the time spent together.  As you
undoubtedly realize, the challenge presented by the specific
```

```
job opportunity now open with the ABC Company sounds extremely
rewarding.
```

Sincerely,

This letter has a lot going for it. It recalls the recent interview. It reviews a subject close to the prospective boss's heart (acquisitions). It describes a contribution of the candidate in the very area the prospective boss is interested in. It reveals the genuine interest the candidate has in the specific job opportunity.

When you contrast this letter with no letter (and most people don't send them), you realize the significant advantage you get with a well-thought-out follow-up letter. One element of the letter above deserves a second comment. The anecdote about the candidate's role in the XYZ negotiation was a direct pick-up from his résumé. It's an anecdote that the candidate has undoubtedly told and retold throughout his interviews. Once your accomplishments are written up, you have an important element of your letters complete and ready for use.

2 / Answers to Ads. Several years ago I asked a special favor of a friend who is a personnel director in a well-known New York company. I asked to look at the responses he received to an ad placed in a major Western newspaper. The personnel director let me see the letters and résumés as they came in, after he had blacked out names and dates to keep identities confidential. Before we discuss the responses, here's the ad that drew them:

> Sales Manager, San Francisco Region.
> Cosmetic experience required. Must have
> knowledge of discount and department
> store distribution. Minimum two years
> sales management experience.

Responses to this ad varied from half-page handwritten notes to a six page tome. The bulk of responses, however, were what I'd call basic transmittal letters, accompanied by a résumé. A typical response to the ad is shown below:

I am writing concerning your advertisement in the _____,
for a Sales Manager in the San Francisco region.

As the attached resume indicates, I've had twenty years of
selling experience. Ten years were in San Francisco. I'm
currently a Sales Manager for a concern selling in this market.

I would very much like to discuss the position you describe
further with you in a personal interview. At that time we
could explore my background in greater detail.

                              Yours very truly,

How dull. How needlessly dull. This letter, and the vast major-
ity of others submitted, did nothing to create a favorable impression on the prospective employer. It did no harm, mind you,
but it did no good either. Contrast the letter above with the one
below. Note how the following letter focuses directly on the prospective employer's problem and the candidate's ability to help
solve it.

Dear Sir:

Your recent ad in the _____ suggests that securing
distribution in San Francisco discount and department stores
is a challenge for your firm. Not surprising since this
market has a reputation for being a tough one for most major
cosmetic companies.

As the attached resume indicates, I have been doing battle
to secure distribution for department store items in the San
Francisco market for the past six years, and with a record
of success. In this regard, you may be interested in the
following:

        Sold seven new fashion accessories to the
        two largest San Francisco department stores
        following my assignment as salesman in this
        market six years ago. These were the first
        items from our company accepted by these
        department stores in over four years.

        Conceived idea for "Cosmetic Buyers Advisory
        Council," an organization designed to serve
        two functions: to bring our company in focus
        with problems faced by cosmetic buyers; to
        improve trade relations with our company.
        Second annual meeting, sponsored by us, took
        place last month.

```
Following promotion to District Manager two
years ago, hired and trained four new salesmen
to call on department stores.  Their combined
sales were 21 per cent ahead of their pre-
decessors the year before.
```

The attached resume spells out in greater detail some of my
other accomplishments, my training and job experience. At
your convenience, I would enjoy meeting with you to review
my background and to learn more about the problems faced by
your company in seeking the distribution necessary for
successfully marketing cosmetics in San Francisco.

Yours very sincerely,

What are the advantages of this kind of letter accompanying
your résumé? There are three things to be gained:

● First, your prospective boss knows you're the kind of a man
who recognizes business problems—and, more particularly, his
problems.

● Second, even before your reader turns a page, he knows
you're a man who can accomplish things he would like to see
accomplished at his company.

● Third, he will realize you cared enough about the opportu-
ity presented in the ad to write a personalized cover letter
rather than a transmittal letter like those he'll see the rest of the
day.

These three advantages make writing this kind of letter worth
the effort. If you don't agree, reread the first and second letters
and ask yourself who got the first call to an interview.

At this point I am sometimes challenged by doubters who
maintain that few, if any, ads reveal needs as completely as the
ad reproduced above. To this I respond: Take a second look
at the executive recruitment display ads in your local paper.
Many do state problems explicitly or implicitly. For example:

● In an ad for a controller: "Must have knowledge of inter-
division accounting procedures for large conglomerate."

• In an ad for production manager: "Three-year-old company seeks mature plant superintendent with knowledge of union negotiations. Must be versed in injection molding, and blow molding equipment."

The secret is to read between the lines and surmise that the conglomerate is having trouble conglomerating, that the young plastics company in the second ad is starting to have labor problems.

It is an unfortunate fact of life that not all executive-recruiter display ads do include a need, and most small-space classified ads do not. That needn't stop you from writing a need-related letter if you adopt the attitude that the vacancy your prospective employer is trying to fill is itself an important need. Consider this alternative beginning to the letter responding to the ad for the San Francisco sales manager:

Gentlemen:

This responds to your ad in the _____ in which
you express a need to locate an experienced Sales Manager
for the San Francisco market. For the past six years, I
have been selling and managing sales people in this market.
You may be interested in several highlights of my selling
career.

There you have it. It couldn't be simpler. The job vacancy becomes the prospective boss's need. And you give yourself a perfect opportunity to highlight your accomplishments up front, to prove you are qualified to fill the position. Your first choice should be a letter which talks to your prospective boss's real problems. Your second, a letter that makes the unfilled job vacancy the need itself.

Several career counselors recommend a different approach in answering blind ads—that is, curiosity-rousing letters. This kind of letter has only one purpose in mind: to whet the appetite of the reader, to literally force him to invite you to his office, where you can present your credentials to him. To write such a letter in response to a classified or recruitment display ad takes a lot of guts. Invariably these ads specifically request a résumé of your experience. But according to the curiosity-rousing formula, you do not include a résumé with your response. Instead, you acknowledge the position you are applying for, provide a synopsis of your work experience without naming the companies you worked with; and provide a list of your key accomplishments. This is an example of a curiosity-rousing letter.

Gentlemen:

This responds to your ad in the April 22 edition of the _____, in which you outlined your need for a creatively oriented director of marketing for a company selling to drug and department stores.

For the past nine years I have been involved in marketing products to these two classes of trade and have worked at three levels of marketing management. Some of my contributions are outlined below:

Organized and directed a four-man marketing department to introduce to the U.S. a new quality line of health-care products.

Programs instituted by this marketing department contributed to these results: two products were in the strong #2 position in test markets just sixteen months after introduction. Two others were in #1 position in the quality segment of the categories in which they compete.

In response to market needs, in one year this marketing group developed and readied for introduction five conceptually new products, the first developed by the company in nine years. These products accounted for 20 per cent of annual volume in the first year.

Earlier in my career, as a marketing manager, took over a gradually eroding $10,000,000 food product. Two years later the brand had its first sales increase in five years (+ 12 per cent). Turnaround reflected a shift in advertising strategy. Sales increase occurred without a price increase and with concurrent reduction in media support.

Created, developed, and introduced the first major line extension for one of the most trusted cosmetic brands in America. Stockholder report states this line extension is the most successful new product ever introduced by the company.

> Introduced a new speciality package for a multi-
> million-dollar brand to increase its consumer
> appeal to a particular market segment. This
> package increased brand sales over $3,000.000
> each year since introduction.
>
> By way of biography, I was graduated with honors from Stanford
> Business School, and with high honors from Michigan University.
>
> I look forward to discussing further details of my advertising
> and marketing experience with you in a personal interview. At
> this time I would enjoy reviewing your specific needs for a
> marketing director in greater detail.
>
> Yours very sincerely,

If your accomplishments are good enough, the letter may do you some good. Whether it gets you in the door, is another question. Why am I a doubter? Simple. I tried the technique. I forwarded a disguised description of my background and accomplishments. In almost every instance, the response was the same:

> Dear Mr. Payne:
>
> Thank you for your letter generally outlining your
> background and contributions. We were most impressed
> with your accomplishments. It's possible we would like
> to meet you once we have more specific information on
> your background. In this regard, please forward a recent
> resume. Naturally, it will be held in the strictest
> confidence.
>
> Yours very truly,

The fact of the matter is this: Curiosity may not be sufficient, in and of itself, to assure you an interview, which is the primary objective of a curiosity-rousing letter. This kind of letter may well increase your work load because you'll have to forward a copy of your résumé, which you could have sent to the personnel director in the first place. In the interim, who knows how many candidates may have entered the prospective boss's office? That frightening thought alone is enough to suggest that the curiosity-rousing letter, instead of a résumé, has a very severe shortcoming.

At this point, you could rebut with the biggest single argument in favor of the curiosity-rousing letter: it doesn't reveal your current company affiliation. That's true. But for the extra time and effort, I'm not sure it's worth while. So let me propose an alternate solution, if revealing your present employer creates problems for you. Prepare your résumé as described in Chapter 3. Identify all the companies you've worked for except your current affiliation. In its place, describe in general terms the kind of company you work for (e.g., one of the top five pharmaceutical houses in the United States). Send your mystery résumé along with a legitimate letter, as described above. This solution provides all the advantages of not revealing with whom you are currently working, and none of the disadvantages of the curiosity-rousing letter.

There is one element in the curiosity-rousing formula that I do subscribe to because it works. *Don't* reveal your salary history when you respond to any ad—even when it's specifically requested. If your résumé is strong enough and your contributions are significantly interesting to your prospective boss, he'll invite you to a personal interview even if you don't reveal your salary as instructed. Then you'll tell him. I've never known of a man who was excluded for not revealing his salary in a letter. Don't be excluded before your interview because of your price tag.

3/ Letters to the man you'd like to work for at the companies you'd like to work at. At some point in your job search you may want to write directly to the companies you would like to work for. When you do write, it will be cold turkey. You won't know if a job opening suited to your experience exists. You won't have a letter of introduction. You'll only know the name of the man you probably would work for if you were hired. That't it. Obviously, under trying conditions like these, your letter has got to be good if it is going to open the door to you. It has got to create excitement from the moment it is opened, build interest in about thirty-three lines.

How will you do it? With a roof-raising, curiosity-provoking letter. The very letter that I recommend *against* when answering ads for a specific job opportunity. And there's a reason for the difference in approach. When you answer an ad, you know your reader has a job need you can fulfill; your letter should be straightforward and direct, focusing on your reader's need and your ability to fullfill it. When you write cold turkey, however, you have to create a need for *you* as a person that your reader "must have working for him." Your letter has to be more dramatic, and, since it's going out to a variety of companies, more general so as to have wider potential appeal. There are four elements it should contain:

● An attention-getting first paragraph that grabs the busiest reader and makes him literally beg to read your letter in its entirety. Here's an example:

```
Everyone in top management said it couldn't be done!  To a
man they agreed you couldn't save this decaying business that
in five straight years had seen five straight sales declines.

To a man, that is, except for one.  So by redirecting sales
through a new class of trade, not thought possible in the
past, I did what top management said was impossible.  For the
first time in six years volume on that item is up!

If your company could use a sales representative who won't
accept defeat -- who keeps trying new inputs until he finds
one that clicks -- you may be interested in some of my other
contributions.
```

And another one:

```
The Wall Street Journal reported today that the heartbeat,
blood-pressure, and life-support systems of our astronauts
can be monitored instantaneously from the moon -- 243,000
miles away.

Can you monitor at a moment's notice the health of the multi-
divisions of your company less than 3,000 miles from your
office?  If today you can't answer "yes" to this question,
you may be interested in the exception control system I
developed for one of the largest retailers in America.  It
pinpoints on one page the significant problems faced on a
daily basis:  inventory imbalances, unprofitable promotional
sales events, store-to-store variations in sales performance,
etc.
```

If this new management tool sounds appropriate to your needs, you may be interested in some of my other contributions that have helped top management to get the most actionable data out of its computer investment.

If you doubt that a dramatic first paragraph can create interest in you, consider this. About five years ago a young man ran a full-page ad in one of the leading advertising trade journals. At the top of the ad, floating in white space, was a coupon. It was marked: "Save $5,000." Below it was a headline that said: "This coupon worth $5,000 on your next creative director." This ad caught the attention of the very advertising agency president that the young man wanted to work for. He sewed up the job he sought at the first interview.

It's not easy to write a dramatic, attention-getting first paragraph. You might want to write several and try them on your friends. Select the one with the greatest emotional impact. Be sure, however, that it relates to the reader's business needs.

• A list of six to eight of your most significant accomplishments, stated in very general terms and in such a way as to create the broadest possible appeal for each. For example, if you developed a new, more economical milk carton for the ABC company, you should refer to your accomplishment as having developed a money-saving container for one of the leading beverage producers in the United States. You'll want to use your curiosity-rousing letter to stimulate the interest of more than just milk-producers. By couching your six to eight accomplishments in general terms, you have a chance to interest beer, soda, and coffee company executives who otherwise might not be interested. By not revealing precisely who or what, you create broader interest in your accomplishments and greater curiosity about you.

• A specific, tangible reference to your education so that the reader knows you're for real. E.g., "graduated from Stanford University in top 10 per cent of class."

• A request for a personal interview.

If your company could use the talents of a creative financial executive with a background of contributions such as those above, I would very much enjoy meeting with you. At that time I would be happy to reveal the specifics of each contribution to you, and to present you with a formal résumé.

If your first paragraph catches a prospective boss's eye (or his secretary's) and your contributions are the kind he's been searching for, he may well invite you in, just to see what this superstar looks like in person. This letter is obviously a long shot but not infrequently worth the effort.

Until now I've suggested a number of job-seeking techniques that you're bound to have some initial doubts about. Unless I miss my guess, this latest suggestion—that you write a dramatic letter directly to the men you'd like to work for at the companies that interest you—seems the most way out of all. I'd agree with you except for one thing: It works for nearly every job-seeker who has a record of accomplishments. Witness the actual results of a cold-turkey campaign conducted just two years ago, as recorded by a job-seeker who tried it much against his better judgment:

Number of cold-turkey letters sent	100
Number of replies	68
From the man letter was sent to	22
From someone in the man's department	8
From personnel department	38
Type of replies:	
Form letter turndowns	43
Personal letter turndowns	17
Offers to meet with job-seeker	
to discuss an opening	8

The nub of the matter is this: the campaign netted eight open doors out of a hundred contacts. Not every job-seeker will fare as well. Some will fare better. Your success depends on how up-to-date your key prospect list is, how dramatic or interesting your first paragraph is (you literally have to stun your prospect's secretary to get your letter onto your prospect's desk), how good your record of accomplishments is, and how well your contributions relate to the reader.

Don't be surprised if your own cold turkey campaign nets as many leads as you get from professional intermediaries in the recruiting business. And if you still have some doubts, consider your investment: ten to fifteen hours developing your list, one to two hours adapting your résumé to a dramatic cold-turkey letter, and $25.00 in stationery and stamps. You can't lose much. So start writing.

4 / Introductions to professional recruiters.   In the next chapter we'll review in some detail the half-dozen kinds of professional —and not so professional—recruitment firms that gain their livelihood by helping people to land the jobs they want. This section deals with the basic letter you'll want to send to almost any of these firms in order to elicit the most aid you can get from them. In brief, your letter to professional recruiters should:

• Transmit your résumé. No good search firm today can work without a résumé. Even if they ask you to fill out their own unique application form in addition, they'll still send out your résumé to their clients.

• Review your key accomplishments. When a professional recruiting firm tries to sell you, or introduce you, to one of its clients, it will need several juicy contributions. If you list them on page one of your letter, they'll be seen and used on your behalf. Equally important, your contributions can get the recruiting firm anxious to sell you instead of the other men it was pushing before your résumé came in.

• Provide a reason why you are leaving. You can't avoid this question when you deal with search firms. They want to tell their clients why you are available. Better for you to give them the real reason than for them to take an educated, or not so educated, guess. If you doubt your letter is important in this respect, consider this. Just last week I learned an agency was sending out to its clients the job-seeker's original letter to the agency along with its own covering note, simply because the original letter so successfully explained why the job-seeker wanted to leave.

• State your current salary, or salary requirement. Inclusion of your salary requirement seems to contradict what was suggested when you answer blind ads or deal direct with companies. True, but there's a reason. Professional search firms want to know how well your salary requirements mesh with the openings their clients have. They feel there's no point introducing you to a company that wants a man earning half what you do. Thus search firms insist on knowing your salary requirement or past salary. Tell them in your initial letter. It saves a return letter asking for this information.

• State your job objective in precise, definitive terms. What titles would you consider? What size company? Where would you be willing to locate? Without this knowledge, search firms are in the dark as to how best to help you. Don't delay their efforts. Include this information.

An example follows of a useful letter to a professional firm involved in personnel relocation:

```
Gentlemen:

For the past five years I've managed the production at a
major company of one of America's blue-chip companies.  The
results of the people I've directed speak for themselves:

    Production up 250 per cent on two products; up
    175 per cent on two others.

    Return on investment in new capital equipment
    recommended by me is under three years.
```

No labor problems have arisen in five years --
following two major strikes prior to my assuming
my current position of plant manager.

Despite these successes, I am eager to relocate with another
firm. This for one reason: my next step up involves a move
to corporate headquarters in another part of the country, and
for personal reasons my family wants to remain in the East.

In relocating, I am seeking a position as director of manufacturing for a medium-sized firm or plant manager for a larger
firm. As indicated on the attached resume, I have experience
in all phases of manufacturing and quality control in the
appliance and electronic industries, and have supervised more
than 500 people. My salary is $35,000. I am however flexible
on salary since the position and location are more important
to me, and I'm sure a reasonable figure can be arrived at if
both parties are happy with one another.

If one of your clients seeks a man with my background, I look
forward to discussing the position with you at your earliest
convenience.

Sincerely,

As you read this complete and thorough letter, two anxious
thoughts may well cross your mind: "If you give away all the information, will the professional recruiter still want to meet you?
And don't you need to sell him in person?"

If your accomplishments and job objective mesh with the professional recruiter's client's needs, he'll have to meet you in
order to recommend you personally. At that time you can sell
him in person on your contributions. It doesn't pay to meet
every professional recruiter. They can't hire you. They can only
place you. And they can't do that until they know of a spot for
you. Then the recruiter will call you in because you are an important commodity worth upwards of $10,000, even more.
They'll want to meet you when they can help you, and themselves.

When you've written drafts of your four basic letters—

1. interview acknowledgments
2. answers to ads

3. cold-turkey company letters, and

4. introduction to professional recruiters—

you've done 90 per cent of the work of letter-writing. From this point on it's a matter of modification and adaptation to suit particular circumstances.

8 | How to Launch Your Better Job Campaign

This chapter is dedicated to every reader who is champing at the bit, each of you who is impatient to get started on his own better job campaign. You have read through seven chapters, and you have yet to talk to anyone who can lead you to the better job you want. This chapter tells whom you should see, when you should see them, and how to reach them.

Before we get started with what is undoubtedly the meat and potatoes of your job-search campaign, let's take up four ideas that can help make the action phase of your job search more effective, four basic thoughts that will add order to what many executives find to be one of the most hectic and chaotic periods of their business careers.

RULES FOR THE ROAD

1 / Establish a specific timetable for getting the job you want. Set down on paper the date on which you intend to complete each phase of your job-search campaign. Plan at the start to hold periodic reviews of your progress. Your initial sessions will concern themselves with the physical work necessary to start the action—the development of appropriate lists, mailing letters, etc. Later your reviews will take on a different and perhaps more important perspective. Then they should help you evaluate the effectiveness of each of the elements of your campaign. Examples: What percentage of the letters you wrote to professional recruiters resulted in interviews? What percentage of interviews resulted in follow-up interviews? What is the general reaction of your prospective bosses to your job objective? Your résumé? Only by reviewing your campaign on a periodic basis can you determine whether or not to make changes that could better your chances for success.

2 / Make a record of your progress.   Even though it may seem like an inordinate pain in the neck, keeping records of everything you do in your campaign will actually save you time and, perhaps more important, help you to make critical campaign decisions. Keep records of professional recruiting firms you've written to, responses received, interviews you've set up. Names of people you've interviewed, particularly if you've spoken to more than one individual in the same company. Position of each man you've interviewed. Mistakes you think you've made along the way. Dates of job offers, if and when you get them, and turndowns too. Ads you've answered.

Why will your records be so valuable? For several reasons:

• There's nothing more flattering to a person who calls than to instantly recognize the organization he's with, how long ago you met him, and the place you met, if it was outside the office.

I'll confess that in the past there were times when I received calls from potential bosses whom I had met just weeks before, and whose names sounded totally unfamiliar to me. After a few goofs, I kept a handy list by the phone of everyone I talked to during my search, and the company each represented. When someone called, he knew he was important to me.

• Knowing exactly when you saw a company last can help you determine its interest in you, help you determine whether you are still a live prospect in its eyes. If, for example, you've had three interviews spaced within two weeks, and then two weeks go by without a call, you had better believe the company has some doubts. Perhaps the job has been redefined. Perhaps a newly met candidate interests the company more. Knowing you are no longer a prime candidate may result in your redirecting your efforts. It's better to know than to live with false hope.

• You give yourself the opportunity to evaluate the effectiveness of each element of your campaign at any point in time. Take letters, for example. Six years ago, a job-seeker sent out two different letters, each to fifty companies he thought he'd like to work for. The first letter yielded seven interview opportunities. The second, two. His first letter apparently worked harder than his second. Not surprisingly, he used the first letter exclusively in subsequent correspondence. If you keep records, you can change your program at any time to make it more effective.

3 / Don't overtax yourself. Do only as much as you can do well.   Nine months ago an executive I coached dropped by. He looked haggard. When I asked if he had a problem, he pointed to his appointment book. Believe it or not, although this executive had a strenuous job, he had squeezed fourteen job interviews into the previous week. Every lunch hour was taken up. It so happened that this man had to travel to get to his interviews, and so he had skipped lunch as a result. He had four 8:00 A.M. appointments, so he skipped breakfast. He had several midafternoon and evening appointments as well. No wonder he was haggard, and hungry to boot. I asked the executive why he made so many interview appointments in such a short period. He explained that in the previous three weeks he had sent out one hundred letters to professional recruiting firms, one hundred more letters directly to companies, and, on top of this, had answered thirty or so newspaper ads. He was overwhelmed with interview offers. Obviously he didn't pace himself well.

There are two reasons why you should not try to do too much in too little time:

• In the first place you could lose your job. If you're out of the office too often, it could be noticed. If your boss knows you're leaving, he might fire you and be done with it.

• In the second place, you can't do a professional job if you're going too fast to keep up. Undoubtedly you'll forego follow-up letters simply because you won't have time to write them. You'll probably have greater difficulty remembering names and faces because you'll meet so many people in so short a time span. Chances are you won't have an opportunity to look up the annual report of each of the companies you interview simply because you are running so fast.

It would be nice if I could suggest the precise number of letters you should write each week. That largely depends on your own available time, the amount of help you have to assist you in the physical details of your campaign, and the interest you generate as a result of your contacts. To be safe, you might start by sending out thirty or so letters to professional recruiters to determine the level of interest in you.

Keep in mind that each interview you set up with a professional recruiter will probably result in one or more interviews with company officials within two or three weeks. Each company you meet with once may want to meet with you again. Your best bet is to let the number of interviews you can reasonably handle guide you in determining the number of letter or phone contacts you should make.

You'll have to experiment. Just take it easy at the start.

4 / Follow up every lead you get.   If you're like most guys, you don't really like blind dates, since you don't know if you'll get stuck with a dog. Most job-seekers feel the same about pursuing blind leads and referrals. Most are dead ends. Others are superproductive. Without benefit of a crystal ball, however, you can't tell which is which. So if you're going to land quickly, you'll have to follow every lead, even if you're convinced beforehand that it's a loser. The least likely person may well be the one to get you your job or lead you to the man who does.

A young financial man I counseled was told by a prospective boss that he didn't have sufficient qualifications for an opening he was being considered for. But the prospective boss was kind enough to suggest that the young man talk to a CPA friend. The young financial guy followed through. The CPA had no job to offer either. But a couple of weeks later one of the CPA's clients asked him whether he knew of a man with precisely the qualifications of the young financial man. The client firm never placed an ad for this job opening because the young financial guy was introduced by the CPA and got the job.

Leads have a way of snowballing. But you have to keep the snowball rolling. Don't overlook any referrals. One further thought on follow-up: If your prospective boss suggests calling back in a week, do it in precisely seven days. Don't take a chance on his being out of town on the eighth day.

5 / *Organize your time in a way that will maximize results.* This means adopting the following priority schedule:

• First, get as many professionals and interested friends working on your behalf as you possibly can. The more people who are on the lookout for the right job for you, the more you multiply the speed with which you land the job you want.

• As a second priority, go after the jobs that are here and now. As soon as you learn of a job opening, no matter how you learn of it, take action to make sure you are considered for the opening.

• As your third priority, seek out opportunities that don't exist until you make them—the long shots. This type of activity has yielded many a job, but (and it's a big but), because this way to a better job has the odds against it, it must take a back seat to your efforts to get a team working for you and to go after the tangible opportunities that are here and now. The balance of this chapter spells out this strategy. It can make the difference between a quick relocation and a long dragged-out battle to get a better job.

PROFESSIONAL RECRUITERS—THE MEN TO GET TO FIRST

Several years ago a building contractor started an addition to my house and, after accepting a check for several thousand dollars, disappeared into the night. Naturally I got hold of a lawyer, who for $200 wrote a compelling complaint and a summons to appear in court. Unfortunately for me, the unscrupulous contractor had vanished and the summons was never delivered. The $200 I spent on the complaint and summons was money down the drain—worthless paper, because the summons was never seen by the man it was addressed to.

Your résumé, the personal advertisement that sells your contributions, is worthless too until it gets into the hands of those executives who need a man like you. Without question, professional recruiters are the most effective means for you to deliver this advertisement. Professional recruiting firms are in business for the very purpose of bridging the gap between your talents and your prospective employer's needs. Not to take advantage of them first could be the single biggest mistake of your job-search campaign.

Who are these firms? How can you reach them? Professional job recruiters range from highly professional, prestige firms to one-man, back-room operations that exist by the grace of Alexander Graham Bell. For the record, here's the roster:

1 / Executive recruiters. The most prestigious of the professional recruiters, these organizations are employed by those companies seeking men to fill vacant executive positions, typically at $20,000 and up. Executive recruiters are generally on retainer but earn additional incentives (up to 25 per cent of your first year's salary) when they place you. Executive recruiters rely heavily on repeat business from the companies they represent and are very thorough in checking on the backgrounds of the job-seekers they discover. Their thoroughness can be a nuisance to job-seekers when they request a detailed written letter to accompany your résumé, or the names of fifteen or so references from the past. This is particularly a nuisance when an executive recruiter requests this information without having a particular client vacancy to fill. But you'd better live with the inconvenience, since executive recruiters can be key people in your life. Typically, executive recruiters themselves have risen in the ranks of business and are personable and highly articulate. Frequently senior company officials retire to the prestige-paneled offices of executive recruiting firms and use their former business contacts to secure the right to represent companies in finding executives to fill key positions.

Because they represent companies, executive recruiters do not promote job candidates. They will put you in contact with a company they represent only if a genuine job opportunity exists. Thus, sending a résumé to an executive recruiter won't often get you in the door of a potential employer. Executive recruiters do maintain active files, however, and it can't hurt to have your résumé in them. Executive recruiters' active files are definitely not circular. I know of a dozen cases in which executive recruiters have located candidates two years or more after they first received the résumé. In most instances it's too late. The candidate is at peace with the world. But not always. An executive recruiter may catch up with you just as you are ready to move again.

Which executive recruiters should you write to? All of them. Why? Because executive recruiters typically are on an exclusive retainer to fill all jobs for the particular company they represent. Thus, when you send your résumé to all executive recruiters, you run very little risk of having your résumé sent to a company from several different sources. At the same time, you broaden the base of companies that might possibly be looking for a man like you. How can you locate those executive recruiters that could help? The most comprehensive list I've seen was developed by the American Management Association and is available if you write to the Management Information Service of the American Management Association at 135 West 50th Street, New York, N.Y., 10020. Executive recruiters seem to merge and change addresses fairly frequently. I suggest you write for an updated list. Last year's may be 20 per cent out of date. A two-year-old list, even more so.

2 | Management consultants. The words "management consultants" and "executive recruiters" are frequently interchanged by job-seekers, and in many respects these two types of firms involved in professional recruiting are similar. There is a big difference, however, and you ought to know about it. Management consultants are primarily in business to solve systems and organizational problems for their client companies. As part of their assistance program, many management consultants do offer their clients a secondary service. That is finding executives for positions that developed as a result of restructuring the organization according to the consultants' recommendations. Management consultants involve themselves in executive recruiting practice in the same way as executive recruiters. They work for the company, not the candidate, and are interested in people only when they have specific job openings to fill. As with executive recruiters, management consultants rarely if ever overlap each other in representing a client company, and you need not fear duplicate distribution of your résumé if you send it out to a number of management consultants. You should recognize in approaching management consultants that, for them, executive recruiting is a secondary service. As such, they are not aggressively seeking people like you. So don't rely heavily on them for results. At the same time it can't hurt to spend eight cents to make sure they know of you in the event that something comes along while you're still looking.

3 / Employment agencies.   There are several different kinds of employment agencies. But there are some characteristics that are common to all. Employment agencies generally don't try to fill positions as high up the organizational ladder as do executive recruiters, and are most often geared to entry-level jobs. So if you earn $30,000 or $40,000 annually, employment agencies probably won't be as helpful as executive recruiters, who place men from $20,000 to $100,000. Don't overlook them, even if you do make a lot. They can still help on occasion.

Employment agencies generally do not work on a retainer basis. They make their money by introducing you to the company that hires you (up to 25 per cent of your first year's salary). Employment agencies rarely have an exclusive contract to fill a job opening. Many seem to learn about the same job openings at the same time, and competition is fierce to be first to introduce a logical candidate. What does this mean to you? If you send your résumé to a large number of employment agencies, you run the distinct risk of having it sent by several different agencies to the company seeking to fill a position for which you are qualified. Overexposure can make you look as if you are desperately seeking a job, an impression you don't want to convey even if you are desperately seeking a job.

A decade ago an employment agency made its money from the employee, who paid a fee to the agency that landed him his job. Today things have changed. Prospective employees balked at paying fees, since they were obviously less well heeled than the corporations that sought to hire them. Employment agencies realized this, and today virtually all feature "fee paid" positions, in which the hiring company agrees to pay the agency's fee. It should come as no surprise that fees are higher now that companies are paying them. You should keep a wary eye out nonetheless, since some hold-out agencies still charge the employee a fee. They are few and far between. Your best bet is to ask if you are not sure. No sense paying to get a job when so many companies are willing to pay for the privilege of finding you. With these generalizations in mind, let's look at three types of agencies you will probably run across.

• Agencies that represent candidates as well as companies. Some smart professional agencies today represent candidates as well as companies. In addition to "filling job orders" (the industry jargon for finding men for positions the agencies have scrambled to learn about), a small number of agencies aggressively promote candidates that they believe have exceptional backgrounds and should be placed easily. Here's how it works: A job-seeker submits a résumé which impresses the agency. The agency invites the candidate to look up the names of the fifty or so companies he would like to work for, and the names of the persons at these companies the man might report to. The agency then phones these companies, singing the praises of the candidate in question. (As a third party it can do this. You can't.) Naturally the candidate has to have some special qualifications that make the agency think he's particularly salable. In instances where the agency represents the candidate, the agency will request a verbal commitment from him that he will deal with it on an exclusive basis while it is promoting his cause. This since the agency gets paid by the hiring company and wants to be sure that its candidate lands at one of the companies it puts him in contact with. The exclusive arrangement assures the agency that it will be paid a fee from some company or other, and this makes the time and expense associated with promoting a particular candidate worth while.

Getting an agency to act as a third-party endorser for you at the companies you'd like to work for can be extremely beneficial in your job search. On the other hand, it's not a sure thing. Frequently the aggressive agency that promotes you will get you interviews with companies that have no immediate openings but are willing to meet you, if for no other reason than to get the agency off the phone. In these instances the interview may be a waste of time. But, since you know how to sell yourself in person, you may well convince a company with no opening that it should make one just to get you. If you think you are exceptional, you should seek out an agency that will act as your spokesman at the companies that you'd like to work for. Ask your friends. Usually the agencies get their exceptional candidates by word of mouth. They don't advertise their promotion service.

• Multi-industry agencies. If an agency limits its sights to a single industry, it obviously limits the number of candidates it will appeal to, and the number of companies it can service. It follows, therefore, that the biggest, most profitable agencies deal with a multitude of industries. Typically, when agencies are large and successful, the staff is broken down by industry, with one man concerning himself exclusively with the potential openings in one or more industries, depending on the size of the industry. Why should this concern you? Because frequently the owners of large and successful agencies hire young, inexperienced, and low-cost staffers to serve as industry specialists. How does that affect you? Very directly. Young, inexperienced industry specialists are less likely to have high-level contacts than mature, experienced professional recruiters who have spent a lifetime developing contacts now in senior positions within the organizational ranks. The young industry specialist is not necessarily inadequate to the task. But, let's face it, more often than not the young specialist has contacts with personnel directors, not vice presidents, and he might thwart your introduction to the right man, despite his good intentions. What should you do with this piece of intelligence? When you talk to employment agencies, evaluate the man who is the intermediary between you and a successful job. If you don't think he'll get you an introduction at the highest possible level, ask him specifically not to make contacts for you with any company without previously calling you. Tell him you want to decide on each company yourself before exposing your résumé. Remember, more often than not several employment agencies will be trying to fill the same job slot. It's likely that you will meet someone from another employment agency who knows of the same opening, and in whom you have greater confidence. It would pay you, therefore, to have personal interviews with the large multi-industry agencies. See who in the organization is promoting your cause before you have your résumé sent out to the wrong man.

• Industry specialists. The smaller, one-or-two-man agencies typically specialize in a single industry. More often than not, the proprietor spent a few years in the industry prior to entering the professional recruiting business. He has an idea of the industry jargon. He knows the industry pulse. The good-to-work-for companies and the bad. He doesn't have to look up *Dun and Bradstreet* to talk about the key people in his field. He knows the cast of characters by heart. Obviously, this type of professional agent can bring more pressure to bear to get you interviews with hiring officials than can the younger, less experienced agency representatives. Your friends should know the names of these industry-specializing agents, since they are the ones who usually get results. Ask them first. If your friends can't help you, you can probably spot these agencies by their ads. Go over four or five back issues of the Sunday classified section. Look through them. Note those agencies that consistently advertise for specific positions in your field. Be wary of those agencies that advertise for general positions in your field, or whose ads are the same each week (e.g., "Senior purchasing jobs—$10–15M"). This type of ad is placed by agencies that are trying to lock up potential candidates without really having positions for them to fill. Send your résumé only to those agencies that consistently have specific jobs to fill in your area, and follow up with a personal interview. In person you'll sense whether or not the agent is capable of making high-level contacts. You want someone on your side who will introduce you to the executive who can hire you, not to the assistant personnel director, who can only forward your résumé.

Don't send your résumé out to several dozen agencies at one time. Limit your contacts to those that appear to be able to help you most. See a half-dozen initially. If they aren't producing interviews after two or three weeks, see a few more. You'll save yourself postage and overexposure.

WHOM ELSE CAN YOU GO TO FOR HELP?

There are a number of nonrecruiting firms that make their livelihood by helping job-seekers to land successfully. Since their ads are frequently interspersed among those placed by management consultants, executive recruiters, and employment agencies, you should know about them. Here's a rundown.

1 / Career consultants. This group of highly successful and profitable firms advertises in the executive recruitment pages that it helps executives to secure better jobs. And for some executives this type of firm provides a valuable service. Career consultants help undecided executives to select the right career goals by means of aptitude and interest tests and personal counseling. They provide individualized assistance in résumé preparation and interview techniques. And they do their job well. It does cost, however. A young, low-priced executive ($12,000) can expect to pay $600 for this service. A senior executive ($40,000 or more) can expect to pay up to $2,800 for counseling. And it takes time. Counseling frequently runs over a period of three months. If you have the time and the money and don't know what you want to do next, there's no question that a career consultant (or executive assessor, as one firm likes to call itself) can be of service to you. From my vantage point, if you've read this far in the book, done your homework, and are anxious to pursue a career consistent with your current background, career consultants are of limited value to you. One word of caution: The advertising by some career consultants is frequently unclear, and if you are not on your toes you might think you are looking at an advertisement placed by an executive recruiter. If you are not interested in career counseling, look for the line buried in the ad in two-point type that says: "Not an employment agency or job placement service." If you do pursue help from a career consultant, a second word of caution: You might be confused by what your career consultant says at your preliminary interview concerning your fee and what it will get for you. To avoid any confusion, let me tell you in advance: Your fee does not guarantee you a job (career consultants are not in the recruiting business, so they don't have positions to advise you of). But your fee is payable whether or not you land a job. Think it over before you sign on the dotted line.

2/ Résumé peddlers.   As you read through the executive-employment section of the paper, you'll probably come across several ads that offer to expose qualified candidates to hundreds of companies with positions that need filling now. The companies who promise this generally have very impressive titles. If you send in your résumé to one of them, you'll undoubtedly be invited to a personal interview. There you'll be told that this firm exposes the résumés of exceptional job-seekers in a new and unique manner. Here's how. The résumé peddler reduces all résumés to half-page summaries (anonymous) and publishes a book of résumés periodically (usually one each month). Some peddlers mail out their résumé summaries to personnel directors at a select list of companies that they've previously asked for an okay to do this. Other peddlers maintain field representatives who make daily calls on personnel directors, carrying with them a binder filled to the brim with résumé summaries. You'll be advised that there is a modest charge for summarizing your résumé and including it in the book. It usually runs around $100. And it's rebatable if one of the companies contacted by the résumé peddler meets you and hires you. From my experience, the résumé peddler has a better deal than you do. He makes about $97 on your résumé summary, while your chances of selling yourself with his résumé summary (which is devoid of all your contributions and is but a mere skeleton of your work experience) seems to be pretty slim.

Recently I learned of a new version of this service which has gone electronic. Not only is your résumé summarized and published anonymously, but a ten-minute videotape interview is made of you. You have a chance to sell yourself to an out-of-town client who is impressed by your résumé. Of course, a videotaped interview has several drawbacks. First, you can only talk generally about your background because you don't know who your prospective employer is or what his specific problems are. Second, this electronic interview obviates the necessity of a meeting in person, which is what you wanted in the first place. I wouldn't place a high priority on the results of résumé peddlers in your job search. But the decision to use them is, of course, up to you.

3 / Professional résumé writers. There are a number of firms that help job-seekers prepare their résumés for a relatively modest fee (usually about $50). These firms employ professional wordcrafters who can take your experience and make it sound good. Each firm has its own résumé format, but most today include accomplishments in some form or other, so that a résumé prepared by such a firm could be of value to you if you are absolutely unable to prepare your own. Several things about the résumés I've seen from these firms concern me, however, and I must pass them along to you.

For some reason, unknown to me, page one always includes a glowing description of the man, using words that sound as if they came from a military commendation. In a résumé, words like these make you seem to be tooting your horn. As you know, it's much more convincing to let your deeds speak for you. Your eloquent description of your own magnificence suggests only one thing: that you might be an egoist.

Most professional résumés look and sound like one another. At one time I received five professionally written résumés from five candidates who answered an ad placed by my firm. Although the men in question had substantially different backgrounds, each sounded as magnificent as the other. In a word, professionally written résumés can be spotted a mile away. In submitting such a résumé, you obviously run the risk of having your prospective boss think you can't write. That's a dangerous shortcoming when you are being compared to other candidates who can.

From my point of view, it's worth sweating a little to write your own résumé. If all fails, you should get help. But you might want to avoid the professional résumé houses that accept mail inquiries. Any résumé-writer who can write your résumé without meeting you has got to be a mind-reader or a charlatan. In my book, he's a charlatan.

4 / Executive marketers.   As the name suggests, executive marketers represent job candidates such as yourself. They are not, strictly speaking, in the professional recruiting business. Interestingly enough, however, some do pick up job orders as they attempt to place the candidates they represent, and in a way executive marketers are like the employment agencies that represent job candidates. But in a big way they are not: Executive marketers make their money by charging the candidates for career counseling, résumé preparation, interview counseling, and, most important, promoting the men they represent to the companies they would like to join. In a way, executive marketers are also like professional career counselors. They provide guidance on how a man should go after a better job. But in two ways they are different. Executive marketers help promote the man to prospective employers (career counselors don't). More important, executive marketers' fees, on the whole, are a great deal less than those of professional career counselors. (It could be one-third as much.) Given a choice between the professional career counselors and the more aggressive and less expensive executive marketers, there should be no question where you should go first.

Frankly, at this point you don't really need either. You know how to sell yourself—in résumés, in interviews, in letters. You know the professional recruiting firms with the here-and-now jobs and the maybe jobs too. By the end of this chapter I hope you'll agree you can get a better job on your own. Why not save the money you could spend on fees? Then spend it in another, more fun way after you get your next job.

5 / Friends and business acquaintances from the past. You don't need me to tell you that your friends and former business associates can be an extremely important source of information concerning currently available jobs and those that might be coming up. So just a couple of points.

Friends who have recently switched positions are an extremely good source of leads. Once they are installed in their new affiliation, they are very happy to review the positions that they weren't interested in, and the professional recruiters who provided the most help.

Men who are looking for new jobs along with you can also be good sources of information. Once they've been turned down by a particular company, there's no reason not to tell you of the job opening. And you might be right for it. In return, tell them of the jobs you're no longer interested in. Don't overlook your competition.

Your address book, business-card file, and out-of-date appointment book are great sources of contacts. The best of us forget some of the people we've met along the way. If you keep old date books (or appointment books) you're bound to turn up a business acquaintance you'd forgotten about. And he may be just the one who knows of the job you want. If you don't keep old calendars, it might not be a bad idea to start doing so. If you change jobs again in three years' time, you'll have a source book waiting for you.

Call your friends. A note won't get them thinking of potential leads half so well as a personal call. And send a résumé, even if a friend can't help you now. Tomorrow he might hear of a job and have your résumé right on his desk.

HOW TO GO AFTER JOBS THAT ARE HERE AND NOW

Once you have executive recruiters, employment agencies, and friends working on your behalf, it's time to go directly after jobs at those companies that just may be looking for you. How can you find them? Obviously, the classified section of your local paper is the place to start. But looking in the local classified section is only a beginning. There are several additional ideas you may want to consider.

• Get hold of back issues of the classified section—eight to ten weeks' issues if you can get them. Many jobs aren't filled in this period of time. It may be that you are the candidate a company has been waiting for. I know of a man who was the ninety-seventh applicant the company considered. It had been looking for nine months before he came along. (My friend laughingly claims he got the job because the company was too tired to look further.)

• Subscribe to the *Wall Street Journal*. The "Mart" section of the *Journal* is undoubtedly the best single source of leads for senior management positions that I know of. If you don't live on the East Coast, you might ask an East Coast friend to send you copies of the "Mart" section of the Eastern edition. It lists more opportunities than the other editions, and if you are willing to move to further your career, you ought to get hold of the Eastern edition regularly.

• Subscribe to *The New York Times* Sunday edition. It costs about $13 per quarter if you live outside of the New York area, and, as such, is a very inexpensive investment in good job leads. When *The Times* is shipped out of New York, it may not have the classified section. (If you check with the local *New York Times* representative, you may be able to arrange to get it.) The *Business and Finance* section is always included, however, and this section contains eight to ten pages of executive display ads each week.

• Read the business pages of your local paper daily. Look for announcements of promotions and appointments. If you spot an announcement of a promotion for someone in your field you might like to work for, write to him. Don't be concerned that you don't know him. Congratulate him on his promotion. Let him know you'd like to work with him if he's thinking about new blood to increase the effectiveness of his operation. Send him your résumé. He may get back to you with an offer for an interview. The worst he can do is turn you down. Why not give it a chance? Don't stall until the executive gets settled in his new job. For some reason or other, newspapers always seem to publish promotions long after they take place. The executive you congratulate may well have been in his current assignment long enough to have evaluated his staff's performance. He may have already decided he needs someone from the outside. And, you may be Johnny-on-the-spot.

• While you're looking at the business pages, note any companies moving into or out of your area. It's a safe bet that companies moving into your area will want mid-management and even senior management people. A quick note to the man you might work for expressing your interest in the company and detailing your contributions couldn't hurt. When companies move out of an area, often people who have been with them for years decide not to move along. If you are willing to move to the new locale, you may well be a prime candidate for a job.

• Look at back copies and current issues of trade periodicals in your field. Most have job opportunities or classified sections in the back. Some ads will be duplicates of those you'll see in the *Wall Street Journal.* Others will be new to you. Before you subscribe, check your local library. Most have the leading business periodicals on file. And they are the ones likely to have ads that interest you.

• Send your answer-to-ad letters with your résumé five to seven days after the ad first appears. A survey by a leading executive recruiting firm revealed that 75 per cent of the total answers to ads were received within four days after the ad's appearance. If you send your letter out on the sixth day, you're a lot more likely to get it seen and noticed. And if your prospective boss has been inundated with letters during the first four days, he's probably going to be in a better mood when your letter comes in with a smaller stack of mail.

BEATING THE BUSHES TO TURN UP YOUR NEXT JOB

In Chapter 7, I suggested you write to the men you'd like to work for at the companies you'd like to work at. Many men have surprised themselves by finding better jobs this way. Once you have talked to the professional recruiting firms and started them working on your behalf, and have written to companies that advertise here-and-now job openings, it's time to beat the bushes. Time to try to promote yourself directly to companies which interest you, even though you have no reason to suspect they are looking for men like you.

How do you go about it? When your cold-turkey form letter is written, have it typed on your personal stationery, using the same carbon-ribbon (IBM-style) typewriter that will be used later to fill in the names and addresses of the men you want to meet. When your letter is multilithed, and the names typed in, it will be hard to distinguish from a personal letter.

The toughest part of this campaign is deciding which companies to write to and whom to contact at each. If you are willing to move, it's not difficult to find lists of potential companies. Six source books, which provide names of most major U.S. companies and their key officers, can be helpful to you:

Standard Directory of Advertisers
Poor's Register of Corporations, Directors and Executives
Thomas' Register
Dun & Bradstreet's Million Dollar Directory
Dun & Bradstreet's Middle Market Directory
Moody's Manuals (Public Utilities / Industrial / etc.)

You'll find at least one of these annually updated volumes at most public libraries, and larger libraries (at colleges particularly) should have all. Of these, the *Standard Directory of Advertisers* is worthy of special note. It is divided by product category or service. If, for example, you are in the appliance business now, and are interested in staying in this field, you'll find the category listing simplifies your legwork.

If you are in a specialized field, you're likely to find a compendium of firms in your specialty by asking the reference librarian. *The Investment Banker, Broker Almanac,* for example, is a useful source book for executives in the securities field. Similar annuals exist in the publishing and advertising-agency fields, and in all probability, in your specialty, if it is not covered by the more general corporation directories noted above.

The real chore is deciding which companies to write to. There's no right way to go about it. You'll have to decide on the criteria for yourself: location, size, primary product, etc. Then you'll have to leaf through one or more of the enormous directories, jotting down names and addresses of those firms that interest you, names of men you might report to. It's a time-consuming job, and there's no valid shortcut that I know of. (The *Standard Directory of Advertisers* does have an alphabetical index in the front, which could help you if you rely on company name only. That could be an undesirable shortcut, however.)

If you exhaust the possibilities in the company directories noted above, you might try writing to industry associations. Large municipal and college libraries should have the *Encyclo-*

pedia of Associations on hand. Your experience in writing to associations should be very favorable. Your letter to the United States Brewers Foundation, for example, is likely to yield a list of all members, the executive officers of each company in the association, and their addresses. Unfortunately, not all industries have active associations, and not all companies belong to the active ones. But, if you can't seem to locate the companies you want to reach by thumbing through the corporation directories noted above, writing to an industry association is worth a try.

If your job search is local rather than national, there are several alternative sources for you in addition to those cited above. The Chamber of Commerce in most major cities maintains lists of local industries. Frequently these are available free. Some are sold at a nominal price. A call to your local Chamber of Commerce, or even a long distance call to the Chamber of Commerce where you'd like to relocate, should provide you with a good source of potential employers. A frequently overlooked source of company names and addresses is the local newspaper in the area in which you wish to work. Newspapers often publish annual industry reviews. If your local paper publishes such an issue, you'll find "Compliments of" ads placed by virtually all major firms in your area. Generally, extra copies of this special issue are available from the publisher for a dollar or two.

There's another overlooked source you should consider—the yellow pages. It may not sound like a very sophisticated list, but on the other hand, it's probably one of the most comprehensive in any locale. Since you're beating the bushes, there's no reason to pass it up if your search is local. A third source of local company names which is often overlooked is a trusted friendly supplier who calls on you in your current position. If you have close ties with a supplier, and can speak to him in confidence, do so. He may have a sales-prospect list of companies in industries related to your own. If you compile a local list of companies you'd like to work for, call each. Ask the switchboard operator the name of the person who holds the title you would report to. Address your letters directly to the man you want to work for. Don't address them to "Office of the President" or "Personnel Director." If you really want to work at a company, you'll take the trouble to find out the name of the man who might hire you. He's the only guy you want to meet.

As you can see from the variety of sources, if you're willing to make the effort, you can develop a lengthy list of companies you might well work for, companies to write directly to. But it isn't easy. You may feel it isn't worth the effort. You may decide to tackle this particular phase of your job search only after you've exhausted the opportunities you develop through executive recruiters and ads. That prerogative is yours. But, don't lose momentum. If the number of interviews you have each week starts to dwindle, it's time to spend nights in the library securing names of companies that you can write to directly. While writing to companies cold turkey seems to be a long shot, it has worked for so many people it would be a mistake not to consider seriously this way to a better job.

9 | Last Things Last

At the end of the "How to Get a Better Job Quicker" course, I ask the class if there are any problems that seem to be left unanswered. Five questions come up repeatedly. Perhaps these questions are on your mind. With the thought that they might be, let's review each:

1/ How do I close the sale? How do I get my prospective boss to offer me the job? I know I'm one of the finalists, but how do I get my prospective boss to actually make me an offer? If you have another job offer on tap, you have one good answer. If you are in this enviable position, let your prospective boss know that you have a concrete offer from another firm, but that you really want to work for him. Ask your prospective boss if his firm can make a decision concerning you in the next two or three days so you can let the other company know. The competition for you should work in your favor. Somehow, the fact that you're in demand makes you that much more desirable.

Unfortunately, for most of us the second job offer isn't in the bag. There are, however, two other good approaches that you should consider trying:

• On your third or fourth interview, when your prospective boss asks you if you have any questions, ask him, "When can I start?" On the surface this may seem like an extraordinarily presumptuous question. And yet, if you ask it with enthusiasm that shows your genuine interest in the job, your prospective boss should not react negatively. He should see by that question that you are caught up in the excitement, the opportunity, the challenge that the job has to offer, and he should be flattered by it. Even if your prospective boss isn't ready to ask you to join his firm, the question shouldn't create a difficult confrontation. Because it's easy for your prospective boss to answer your question without feeling put-upon. He might, for example, say, "Well, we haven't really selected the man yet and we are still interviewing several, so I can't tell you when you could start—if you are the man that we finally select."

On the other hand, if your prospective boss is genuinely interested in you, and you ask a question like "When can I start?" there is a good likelihood he'll say to you, "When can you join us?" In a word, you can help him to be certain you're the man he would like to hire.

Even with this reassurance, some of you will have strong reservations about such an approach. If you're truly concerned that the "When can I start?" question is too presumptuous, consider the parallel to a salesman closing a deal. A good salesman doesn't say, "Would you like to take this deal?" at the end of his pitch. A good salesman avoids difficult questions that require a yes or no answer. Instead he lets his customer answer an easy question like, "When would you like the deal shipped?" Your situation is quite the same. When you ask your prospective boss, "When can I start?" you're helping him to bypass a difficult question and to get to a much easier one. A word of caution. This approach won't work well on your first or second interview. You have to be pretty darned sure that the company you're interested in is interested in you. You've got to ask your question at the right opportunity. And that's on your third or fourth interview. When your prospective boss says, "Do you have any further questions," ask the one that counts.

● A second "close" that works well—even on your first interview—is this: "I'm convinced this is the job I want. What more do I need to do to convince you I'm the man for the job?" This question could lead your prospective boss to give you a special written assignment to "convince him" in one or more areas where he's not convinced you're the right man. And that's a great opportunity, if he's not yet convinced. On the other hand, it may lead your prospective boss to say to himself, "I really need no further convincing. This man is the right man for the job." In which case you're likely to get a job offer. This question also avoids a direct confrontation. If your prospective boss isn't ready to hire you, he can always say, "We won't need anything more from you at this time. You've told us enough to judge you along with the four other men we're looking at. We'll get back to you soon."

2 / How do I get the salary I want? Earlier in this book it was recommended that you avoid talking about salaries until you've been offered the job. You should try to convince your prospective boss you're the only man he wants. Then, when you talk salary, you have a much better chance of getting what you want. Sooner or later, however, in every job search you'll have to talk salary. It is, after all, the cement that binds. The real question, then, is this: Will the company that wants you pay what you want to make? In most job situations, you should have a pretty good idea of what the job pays before you arrive on the scene. Executive recruiters and employment agencies are frank about the salary range. Similarly, many ads include salary "up to" statements, although some do not. What you really want to know is how to get paid at the top of the range.

There are several things that you can do to help maximize your compensation.

● You have already done the first thing by holding off your discussion of specific salaries until the very end. Your prospective boss has resolved to hire you rather than your competition. He has already decided in his own mind you are the top man and probably worth the top dollar.

● Second, let your prospective boss talk salary specifics before you do. If, after offering you the job, he asks you what you want to make, why not turn the situation around? Why not ask your prospective boss what salary he has in mind? Put him in a position of trying to make the sale. By the time your prospective boss has offered you a job, he wants you. Put him in the psychological position of trying to get you. Chances are that he'll offer you the maximum dollars in the job's salary range.

● If the salary offer doesn't match up to your needs, use a comparison to help your prospective boss realize the problem. Obviously, the best comparison is a salary offer from a competitive firm. If you're lucky enough to have one, you might let your prospective boss know at this time in a nice way. For example:

> As I told you, I have been talking to several companies. Yours is my absolute first choice. On the other hand, one of the reasons I'm leaving my current firm is to improve my financial situation. In considering job opportunities, I have to take into account that I have an offer for $2,000 more. I'll think the situation over during the next few days. If perchance there's a way of arranging the budget so that your job could pay more, I certainly would appreciate it if you would let me know. It would make my decision easier!

If you don't have another job in your back pocket, you can still help your boss to see your problem with a comparison to what you're now making. This is the kind of thing you might say:

> Thanks very much for your offer. I'm really glad that I turned out to be your first choice, because, as you know, your company is my

first choice. But I'll be candid with you and tell you that I do have a problem. When I decided to leave my current firm, I established a goal for myself of securing a job that pays 20 per cent more than I now make. Money's really a major reason why I'm leaving. At this point in my job search, I don't think I should move away from this goal. So I have to let you know my problem. I recognize it is really mine. But if perhaps your budget might be adjusted, I hope you will let me know so that we might discuss this further. For now, as much as I appreciate your offer, it's not consistent with my needs. I'll have to think it over during the next few days.

The first half of your strategy is, of course, to make the salary you want seem reasonable. Reasonable by virtue of the competitive situation. Reasonable by virtue of the fact that one normally expects to make more in a move. The second part of your strategy is to give your prospective boss time to think it over. Time to reflect on whether or not he wants to go to his second-choice candidate, or begin the search again. By giving your prospective boss time to think, you're making it easier for him to rationalize an increase. And chances are greater you'll get what you want.

3 / How much time do I have between saying yes and joining my new firm? Most job-seekers expect prospective employers to pressure them into joining a company immediately—to leave their current companies in the lurch, to take no time off before they join their new employer. The amount of pressure that's applied to men who've said "Yes" is amazing. It's understandable that a company that has been searching for nine months or a year would want you right away. But it's unreasonable. You should be given the opportunity to wind up your business at your current firm, to take a well-deserved vacation. You can easily take six weeks between saying "Yes" and joining your new firm—a minimum of four. Two weeks' notice to your current employer, and two weeks for you to unwind and relax. And you really owe it to yourself to do just that. To take a vacation. To look at new surroundings. To think of no work at all. So that when you join with your next company your mind is fresh and your senses are keen, you are ready and willing to tackle the new assignment. As you move up the organization chart, two weeks' notice may be too little. You may want to give four. Hence your prospective employer should expect to wait six weeks. There is no doubt that this delay will frustrate your prospective boss. He wants you now. He needs you now. But remember, your best chance to unwind completely is between jobs. Take the opportunity. Don't let it slip through your hands. Whatever you do, don't leave your former company on a Friday and start to work at the new company the next Monday. Every man I know who has done this has regretted it. A weekend is not enough time for yourself. And, since it may be a year or eighteen months before you can get away on a vacation from your new company, take the time between jobs for yourself. Don't succumb to the pressure. You deserve to take a break.

4 / What happens if I get a better job offer after I've accepted with one company? It occurs with greater regularity than you'd think. People accept job offers with one company. Then, if they get a better opportunity with another, they renege on the first. The decision as to whether you renege on a job offer that you've accepted must be yours. It's hardly something that could be recommended in this book. Nonetheless, it might be worth while to examine the implications of reneging, in case you find yourself in a situation where you are giving considerable thought to this action.

There are two circumstances that might bring you to a decision to switch your allegiance even before you join a company. The first of these is the situation in which you accept a job simply because you need bread and butter on the table. You know the job isn't what you want. It doesn't conform to your job objectives, near- or long-term. After you accept this job, and before you start work, another job appears on the horizon. This one is just what you want. It is in tune with both your short- and long-range goals. I personally think you would be remiss not to take the second opportunity, since it offers you so much more than bread and butter. In this instance, it seems to me that talking frankly to the people at the bread-and-butter company won't be as traumatic as you think. If you refer to the job objective stated on your résumé and your long-term goals (if you talked about them in your interview), the people at this company should agree with you that your decision is a wise one. While they will probably hold your decision against you for a while, I am sure in the long run the first company will agree that your change of heart is best for you and for it.

The second reason why you might think about reneging is different. Simply stated, the second company offered you more money. If money is the only differential, and both first and second opportunities satisfy your career goals, think twice before you renege. The people at the first company might well be vindictive. They might try to get in touch with the second company. They most assuredly would get in touch with the recruiting firms they deal with. Your reputation could be tarnished. Even if you disregard the moral issue of reneging after accepting a job offer, it would seem to be in your best interest to join the company you accepted first, even at the loss of a few dollars. Unless it's a question of career objectives being much better fulfilled by the second company, I'd think twice before saying no once you've said yes.

At this point you may well ask, "Is there any way in which I can get the first company to up its ante once I get a second job offer which pays more?" The answer to the question is simple: "No." Even if you were to speak to the first company concerning the salary offer of the second, and were able to squeeze a few extra bucks from the first, it wouldn't be in your best interests to do so. Chances are your new boss would think a great deal less of you. You would certainly not be stepping off on the right foot in your new affiliation. This situation is sort of like that of the man who sold a house for $45,000 on a Wednesday, and a real estate agent phoned him on Thursday and asked if the house was still for sale. When he told her "No," she said, "Too bad be-

cause I have a buyer who will offer you $50,000 for your house."
So be it. The house is no longer yours.

Is there a simple way to avoid the frustration described
above? Yes. When you've accepted an offer with one company,
forget your job search. Plan your vacation. Finish up your current work. And if you still find yourself with time left over, call
your next boss. Ask him if there's anything he'd like you to read
before you join his company. Get totally involved with your
next job. You won't have time to be frustrated.

*5 / When is the best time to talk about fringe benefits and other
special arrangements?*   Most fringe benefits, such as stock purchase plans and stock options will be discussed when your boss
talks turkey with you concerning your financial package. But
there are several extras that might get overlooked. These include a cost-of-living allowance, should your job require you to
relocate six or nine months after you join, to another, more expensive city. A second key extra is moving expense. Most companies pay moving expenses of employees who join from a considerable distance. Not all do, however. If you want the
company to pay moving expenses, or a cost-of-living allowance,
the time to discuss it is when you discuss your financial package. If you haven't made arrangements then, it's a hairy task to
reopen the discussion at a later date. A cross-country move
could cost your firm $5,000. No one likes a $5,000 surprise. Be
sure to write down all the items in your financial package that
you want to cover in your negotiations. When the time comes to
discuss finances, be sure you touch upon each.

Be well thought of wherever you go. In the period that follows your acceptance of an offer you might easily forget the
companies that didn't offer you a job. It's not surprising that you
would. Trying to finish up your job at your current company,
getting organized for a vacation, and getting yourself in the

mood to join a new company can keep you hopping. Since many people do forget, one final suggestion: Be remembered positively by the companies you didn't join and the professional recruiters who worked with you as you searched for the job you wanted. Send a form letter to all those companies, executive recruiters, and agencies who have written to express an interest in you, and particularly to those whom you've met. Let them know where you are going. Express your thanks for their aid. This is obviously a low-priority task. But I'd recommend it to you. Not every new job works out. Not every job that seems better on the surface is really better. And a year or two after you join a company, you may be looking again. Your folder with a thoughtful letter may still be in the active file. When and if you go looking again, you will be very well thought of for the courtesy you showed, since so few people show it. It's nice to be remembered nicely. What's more, you never know if a professional recruiter may come up with a great job opportunity and want to see you a year or two after you start your new job. It will give you a nice feeling to know that he knows where to reach you. If there ever is a next time, you'll have a head start on getting a better job quicker.

10 | A Special Word to the Man Out of Work

If you've ever been fired (and I have) you know the day it happens is not the most auspicious in your life. Even though you may feel you were fired unjustifiably, it stings nonetheless.

The sad fact is that while the day you are fired is a heartache to remember, the days that follow can be even more depressing. Only the numb of mind could fail to feel the financial bind, the sinking feeling that comes when you know that the well must soon run dry, that the usual biweekly replenishing source has been cut off.

And no man, no matter how good he is, can fail to ask himself why he was fired, to assess from time to time what went wrong. What could have been done differently. How things could have worked out, had other ways been tried. Even if your boss tells you it's not your fault (as my boss told me when my position was eliminated), you can't help blaming yourself. The proudest of us feels tarnished on some days; the original lustre will never be the same.

Then the loneliness sets in. The office faces and voices, so familiar they have become a subconscious part of you, are suddenly gone. The phone no longer rings. The pretty secretary is no longer there with coffee and a smile. To many executives, and perhaps to you, the loss of momentum is the source of your greatest frustration. Every day for the past five years, or ten, you've been caught up in a money-making track meet, overcoming obstacles and pushing yourself to meet deadlines. Then, in an instant, the rhythm of business vaporizes. The only pressure left is that which you impose upon yourself to get a new job.

And in one way we amplify the depression for ourselves. The natural batten-down-the hatches feeling leads most of us to give up gardeners and dinners out, theater tickets and baby sitters, cleaning help and other commonplace luxuries. The bitter pill of being fired is more bitter for the act of self-preservation.

To those of you who, like me, have been fired, these thoughts:

● Don't lose heart. When you are fired, you are automatically initiated into a prestigious club—a club that includes on its rolls some of the most brilliant, successful men the world of commerce has ever known. I know the president of a billion-dollar firm who got the ax. Now he's president of a two-billion-dollar firm. I once worked for a multimillion-dollar corporation whose president proudly told me on the day we first met that he never would have joined his present company if he hadn't been booted from a position with this company's toughest competitor. That president considers his firing to be the luckiest break of his business career. Whatever you do, don't think your situation is unique. If you ask your ten closest friends, chances are good that at least one has pounded the pavements at some point during his business career. In short, no good man ever succumbed fatally to being fired. You won't either. If you still feel down on your luck, remember this: Not more than one in twenty job-seekers takes the time and trouble to prepare himself to get a better job. But you did. You know the rules of the road. You have the inside track. Soon you'll look back on your current circumstances as though they were ancient history. And you'll be all the wiser for them.

• Hold on to your office routine. Whatever you do, don't sit at home. For nearly every adult day of your life, you've gone to the office. Keep going. Even if you don't have your old office. Where should you go? It's possible your former employer will let you occupy space somewhere in the recesses of his building, so that you have a place to work out of. If not, a friendly supplier might make room for you. When you join another firm, you'll probably be in the same industry. It would pay a supplier to befriend you now. Later you'll repay his kindness. He knows it. If your list of suppliers doesn't turn up space and a phone, check with your close friends who own their own firms, or who are officers in larger concerns. Chances are you'll come up with desk space, part-time secretarial assistance, and your name on the telephone list. If you can't find office space, still get out of the house. The public library is public. Occupy a desk every day and keep your files in your briefcase. Don't worry about phone calls. You don't get too many when you're between jobs. If you check in with your wife at home two or three times a day, you can get back to whomever wants you. Don't worry about the delay. Whoever calls will probably think you're out on an interview, and that's better than being thought of as being home in bed.

Two more points regarding office routine:

1. No matter how little work you have to do, don't take a vacation. In the first place you'll lose your job-search momentum. You're in business for yourself when you're between jobs, and your number one order of business is to get a new job. In the second place, you could be away when the very job you want breaks. I know a man who delayed his second interview by a week. When he showed up the next Thursday, he learned the job had been filled on Tuesday. After you have a new job, take off. You'll enjoy it more when you have lined up a position, anyhow. And you won't worry how you're going to pay for the vacation.

2. Dress as though you had been promoted, not fired, even if you have to polish your own shoes. No matter how tight

your budget, invest in clean, pressed suits and heels that are not run down. You need to convey an aura of success in order to get the better job you want. Just as important, when you are well dressed you'll feel psychologically at your best. You can't keep your shoulders erect in a slouchy suit. When you're looking, only you should know it.

• Keep the pressure on yourself. Until the day the pink slip came, there weren't enough hours in the week to complete all the business tasks you wanted to get done. When you're out looking, you obviously won't feel the same kind of pressure. You might succumb to the Well-I-might-as-well-enjoy-my-unemployment minimum work pace. Don't. Or your job search may well last longer. At this point, let me anticipate your inevitable question, "What on earth can I do all day?" Plenty. Let's assume you've written your contributions list, your résumé, your form letters, that you've developed your list of a hundred companies you want to go after. Even with all that out of the way, there's a great deal you might do. Here are some suggestions:

1. Develop a second list of a hundred companies that you might work for. If the first list isn't paying off, you should develop new objectives before you start on your second list.

2. Develop an employment agency follow-up campaign, a short-form letter, or postcard, preferably one that will really catch attention. Send a different letter or card each month, asking the agencies what they've done for you lately. You don't want to be forgotten as agencies pursue the placement of newer candidates.

3. Review your résumé critically. After eight weeks of interviews, you may well find elements of your résumé that require amplification or deletion. Tighten your résumé up. It can't take more than a few hours. And it could save you a few months of searching.

4. Develop a list of long-forgotten contributions. This true story explains why. An advertising executive I know re-

membered that twelve years before his first agency work he had contributed the basic idea for a direct-mail campaign. Although he hadn't been involved in direct mail since then, he answered an ad seeking a direct-mail advertising manager. He eventually got the job. He never would have applied if he hadn't probed the recesses of his background.

5. Tape some facsimile interviews. Listen to your voice. You may well want to change your answers or your intonation.

6. Write an objective memorandum to yourself on how you would have changed your previous operation to make it more successful. A carefully written memo will help you to define the perimeters of the problem more succinctly than daydreaming about what went wrong. If, later on, you read it from time to time, it may actually help you to succeed on your next job.

7. Visit other cities you might work in. Read the last eight weeks' classified sections at a public library. You might find a number of jobs that were not known to you in your current base of operations.

8. Read other books on job search. They may provide some new ideas that might work for you. And reread this book. The best of us will not recall all the techniques and suggestions with a single reading. A second review may turn up just the thought you needed to make your job campaign quicker and more effective.

• Don't dwell on your weaknesses. Any man who has been fired tends to review what went wrong. It's only natural. How much you think about the past, and how you think about it, however, can affect your ability to sell yourself successfully in person and on paper. If you put yourself in a rotten frame of mind by deciding you were fired because you were no good, you can be sure that your depression will work against you in your interviews. Your best bet is to limit the time you think about the past. If, for example, you promise yourself to think about the past only on Monday mornings, turn off your conscious reverie when the past creeps into the crevices of your mind on Tuesday. Instead, work on something productive like a follow-up letter. And when Monday morning's introspective session rolls around, dwell on what went wrong for only a short time. Then get that memo outlined on what you'll do on the next job to avoid the problem again.

• Share your search campaign with a friend. Getting a better job is a lonely assignment. This is doubly true if you are out of work. Whatever you do, don't put yourself in needless solitary confinement. Share your progress, your burdens, and your successes with one or more business associates or friends you can see on a regular (once a week or so) basis for lunch or during the day. You'll find they enjoy your confidence, are flattered by your asking them for counsel. They are likely to have ideas you haven't explored. Whatever you do, don't place yourself in the role of a pariah simply because you are out of a job. Your true friends are your friends, whether you're working or not. When you get a better job, break out the champagne. Your friends will enjoy it more for having helped you along the way.

Let Uncle Sam
Help You
in Your Job Search

The other day I had lunch with a friend who happens to be one of the foremost tax lawyers on the West Coast. It's not surprising that the conversation turned to a topic of interest to us both: the tax implications of job search. Here in a nutshell is what my friend told me:

> As of the 1970 tax return, if you are successful in your search, the government will help you pay your related expenses. If you aren't successful, it won't.

Let me amplify this thought further. If you get a new job, you may declare your out-of-pocket expenses on your income tax return as "business expenses not paid for by your company." This is done as one of the miscellaneous expense items toward the end of your tax form. If you are out of work for the year, however, you can't declare the costs incurred in trying to get a job. If this sounds to you unfair to the jobless, then you share my view. The fact remains that this is the current law. The same seemingly unfair situation exists for businesses that are just starting up. If you as a businessman put out thousands of dollars in developmental costs in a year and don't derive any income, you can't declare your loss. Once you get the business going and have an income, however, then you can declare your costs. That is, if you have enough financial backing to remain in business until you are successful.

One other point of law you should know. You can't declare the expenses you incur in getting your first job—only the expense you incur in switching jobs. I'm not sure why the government discriminates against the first-time job-seeker, but, according to my tax lawyer friend, the tax laws prohibit a new job-seeker from declaring expenses resultant from his first job search. Happily, most of the people who read this book will be switching jobs and will qualify with this aspect of the law.

If you plan to declare your expenses (and you should), keep accurate records. Keep your bills for stationery and résumés. Your mileage incurred as a result of interviews. Parking receipts. Plane fares for which you are not reimbursed by prospective bosses. Toll calls. Postage. (You'll have to make out a receipt before you go to the post office.) While these items individually may seem small, in aggregate they can add up to a substantial figure. You might as well let Uncle Sam pay his share (your tax percentage), since the law says he is willing to do so. Naturally, the major fees you pay to career counselors and employment agencies are expenses you may declare, if you get a job. Though, as I said earlier, you are better off not incurring these expenses at all. Uncle Sam pays only his fraction (your income tax percentage). Why not avoid these costs 100 per cent if you can?

ONE CAUTION: This short appendix is included so that you don't overlook the opportunity of tax relief on your job-search expenses. If you are unsure of an item, see your tax accountant or tax lawyer. Be sure.

ABOUT THE AUTHOR

An eminently successful executive, teacher, and writer, Richard A. Payne has, in remarkably few years, compiled an impressive record of successes in a number of challenging fields. Born in 1934, he graduated Magna Cum Laude from Princeton University after which he went on to earn an M.B.A. from the Harvard Graduate School of Business Administration, graduating in the top 10 per cent of his class.

A former account executive at J. Walter Thompson and Ogilvy & Mather, two of the nation's largest advertising agencies, Mr. Payne has also been a product director for Johnson & Johnson, a group product manager for Chesebrough-Pond's, and a group product manager for the International Paper Company.

Mr. Payne is the founder and present director of the "How to Get a Better Job Quicker Course," an intensive, proven program consisting of four 3-hour seminars designed to supplement the material presented in this book. This course is offered in major cities throughout the United States under the auspices of Critical Path Systems.